GRATITUDE JOURNAL

By
MIKE BHANGU

BBP
Copyright 2019

Copyright 2019 by Mike Bhangu.

This book is licensed and is being offered for your personal enjoyment only. It is prohibited for this book to be re-sold, shared and/or to be given away to other people. If you would like to provide and/or share this book with someone else, please purchase an additional copy. If you did not personally purchase this book for your own personal enjoyment and are reading it, please respect the hard work of this author and purchase a copy for yourself.

All rights reserved. No part of this book may be used or reproduced or transmitted in any manner whatsoever without written permission from the author, except for the inclusion of brief quotations in reviews, articles, and recommendations. Thank you for honoring this.

ISBN: 978-1-988735-53-5

Published by BB Productions
British Columbia, Canada
thinkingmanmike@gmail.com

This gratitude journal belongs to:

_____

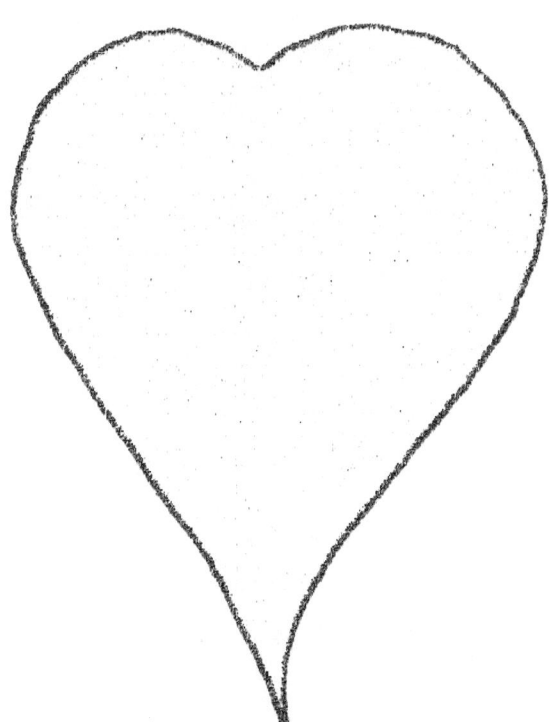

"Gratitude can transform common days into thanksgivings, turn routine jobs into joy, and change ordinary opportunities into blessings." - **WILLIAM ARTHUR WARD**

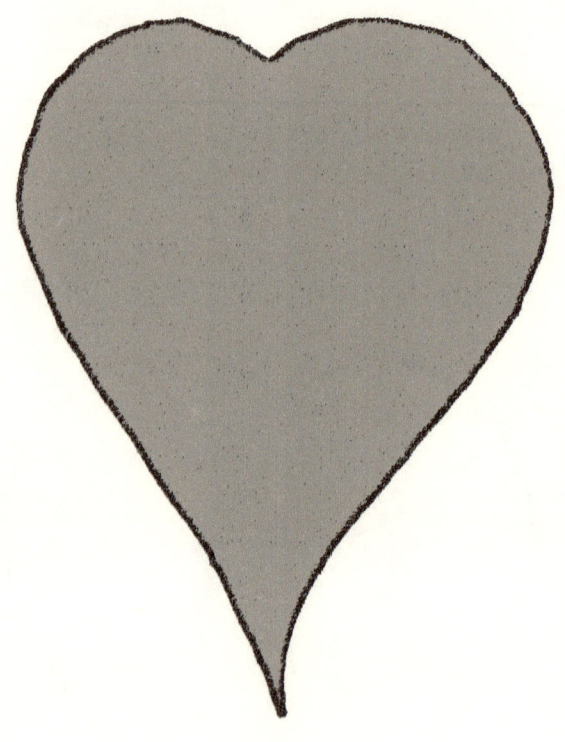

INTRODUCTION

Thank you for purchasing this journal. I am truly grateful and I hope this journal helps you achieve your goals.

This gratitude journal is easy to use and requires less than five minutes daily. Each morning complete a page. There are 90 pages for 90 days. Each page asks you to write down three things that you are grateful for, and to draw the phrase "Thank You". It's simple and the rewards are immense. At the end of 90 days, you'll be asked to write a brief gratitude letter.

The power of gratitude can change a person's life. This is because gratitude creates a favorable metaphysical presence. Each person has two natures: the metaphysical and the physical. The metaphysical aspect influences how a person feels, thinks, behaves, etc. Moreover, the invisible nature influences the type of interactions, experiences, and outcomes a person attracts. A grateful attitude will generate a metaphysical vibration that enhances interactions, experiences, and outcomes. And a grateful attitude will improve how a person feels, thinks, and behaves.

Writing three things of gratitude and drawing the phrase "Thank You" daily, and writing a gratitude letter, will nurture a favorable vibration.

The things you are grateful for can be big or small. Don't stress. You can be grateful for a dream, your breath, the sunshine, the rain, your favorite color, a glass of almond milk, or a pair of clean socks. It's all good. There's always something to be grateful for.

As a reward for completing 90 days of gratitude, at the end of this journal, I share a simple technique designed to help increase abundance. This method I learned from a world-renowned yogi. Supposedly, Steve Jobs utilized this technique. Before a person can practice this method, an individual should vibe right and 90 days of genuine gratitude will generate a favorable vibration.

If you're wondering who I am, my name is Mike Bhangu and I am a spiritual specialist and philosopher. I've spent over twenty years studying and researching the many different theologies, spiritual houses, and world philosophies. In this time, I've discovered core understandings that will enhance a person's spiritual evolution and journey to break the matrix. I've written over ten nonfiction books sharing my discoveries. One fundamental understanding is the power of gratitude.

Gratitude can be difficult to practice. We too often allow the mind to drift toward the negative. Sometimes, this becomes habitual. Daily writing three things that you are grateful for, daily drawing the phrase "Thank You", and writing a gratitude letter will help break the cycle of negative thought and will assist the mind drift toward the positive. The power of gratitude is life changing. Try it!

> "Gratitude makes sense of our past, brings peace for today, and creates a vision for tomorrow."
>
> **- Melody Beattie**

Date: ____/____/____   Day: 1

AN ATTITUDE OF GRATITUDE.

Today, I am grateful for:

1. _____

2. _____

3. _____

In the box below, draw **"Thank You"**. Allow your creativity and love to flow, and it's okay to doodle. ☺ While you draw, genuinely thank the things you are grateful for.

EXAMPLE:

"Gratitude is not only the greatest of virtues, but the parent of all." - **MARCUS TULLIUS CICERO**

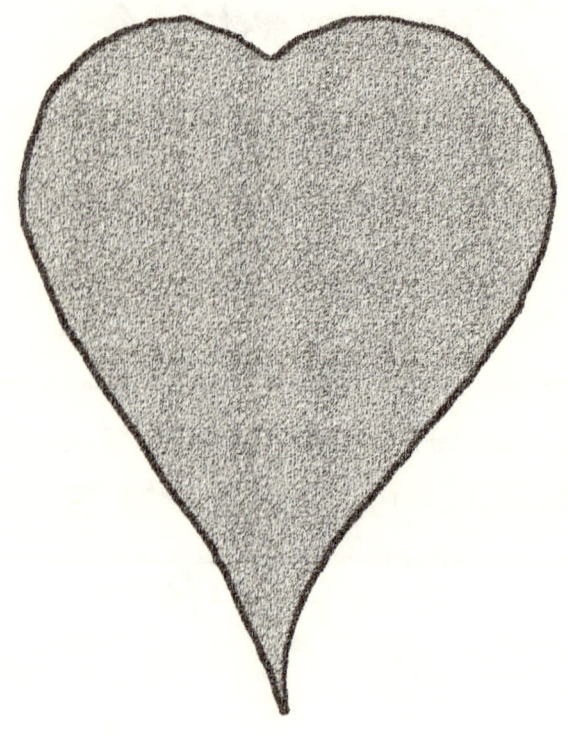

Date: ___/___/___ Day: 2

AN ATTITUDE OF GRATITUDE.

Today, I am grateful for:

1. _____

2. _____

3. _____

In the box below, draw **"Thank You"**. Allow your creativity and love to flow, and it's okay to doodle. ☺ While you draw, genuinely thank the things you are grateful for.

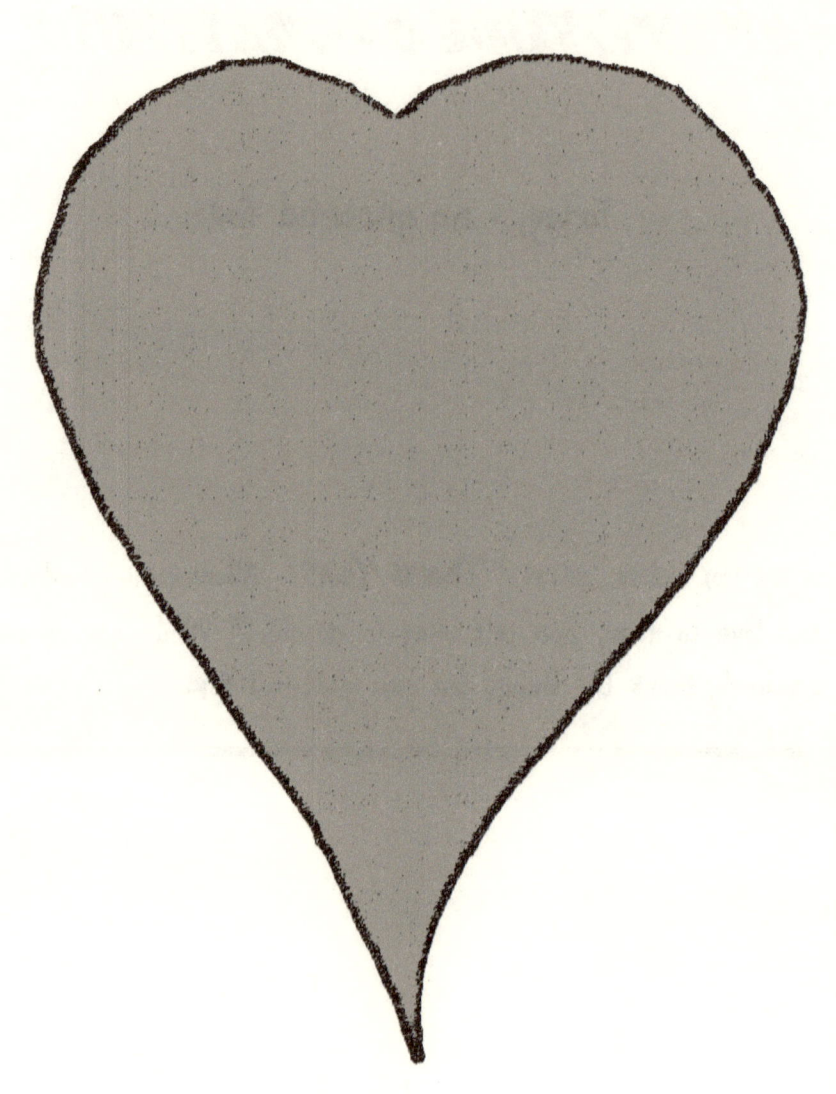

Date: ___/___/___   Day: 3

AN ATTITUDE OF GRATITUDE.

Today, I am grateful for:

1. _____

2. _____

3. _____

In the box below, draw **"Thank You"**. Allow your creativity and love to flow, and it's okay to doodle. ☺ While you draw, genuinely thank the things you are grateful for.

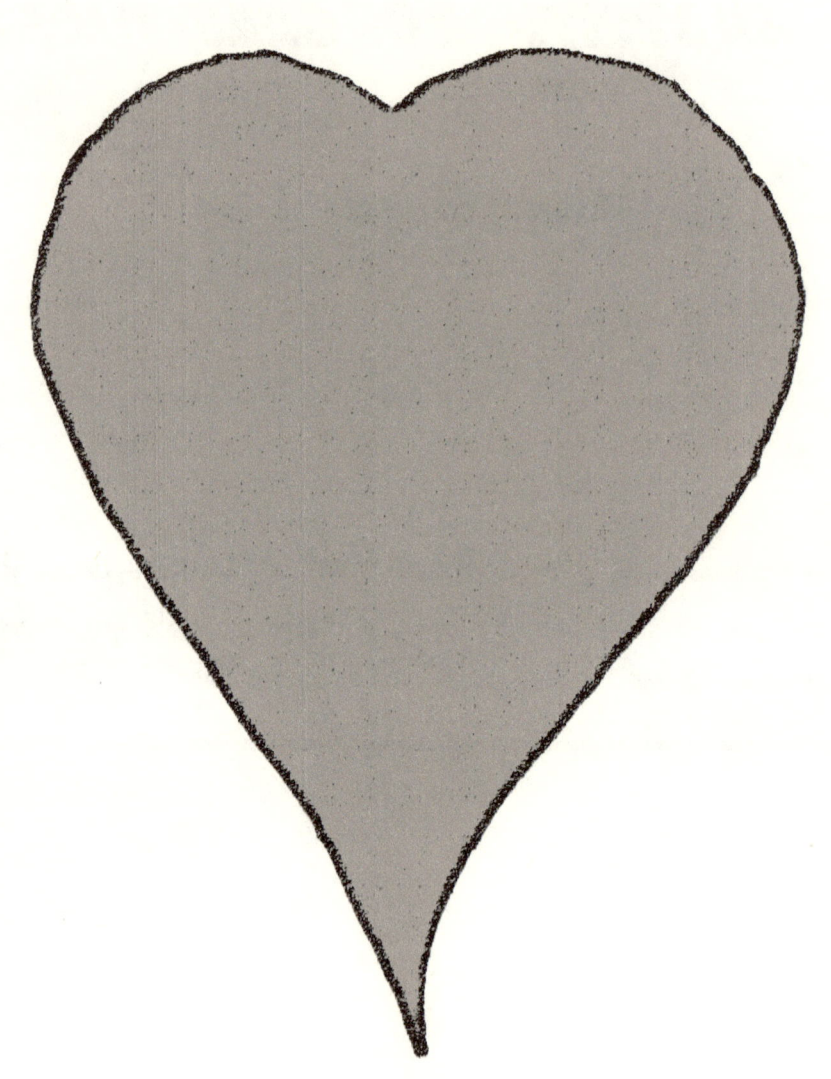

Date: ____/____/____   Day: 4

AN ATTITUDE OF GRATITUDE.

Today, I am grateful for:

1. _____

2. _____

3. _____

In the box below, draw **"Thank You"**. Allow your creativity and love to flow, and it's okay to doodle. ☺ While you draw, genuinely thank the things you are grateful for.

"Appreciation can make a day even change a life. Your willingness to put it into words is all that is necessary." - **MARGARET COUSINS**

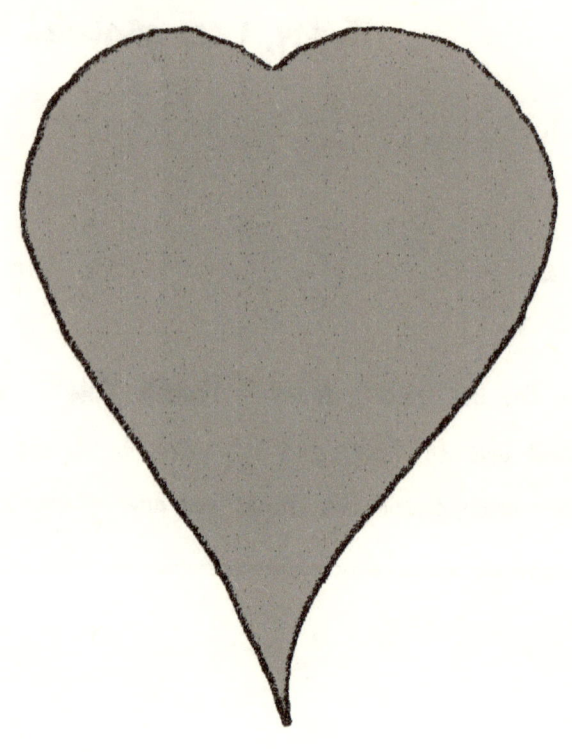

Date: ___/___/___   Day: 5

AN ATTITUDE OF GRATITUDE.

Today, I am grateful for:

1. _____

2. _____

3. _____

In the box below, draw **"Thank You"**. Allow your creativity and love to flow, and it's okay to doodle. ☺ While you draw, genuinely thank the things you are grateful for.

Date: ___/___/___   Day: 6

AN ATTITUDE OF GRATITUDE.

Today, I am grateful for:

1. _____

2. _____

3. _____

In the box below, draw **"Thank You"**. Allow your creativity and love to flow, and it's okay to doodle. ☺ While you draw, genuinely thank the things you are grateful for.

Date: ____/____/____   Day: 7

AN ATTITUDE OF GRATITUDE.

Today, I am grateful for:

1. _____

2. _____

3. _____

In the box below, draw **"Thank You"**. Allow your creativity and love to flow, and it's okay to doodle. ☺ While you draw, genuinely thank the things you are grateful for.

"I would maintain that thanks are the highest form of thought; and that gratitude is happiness doubled by wonder." - **G.K. CHESTERTON**

Date: ___/___/___   Day: 8

AN ATTITUDE OF GRATITUDE.

Today, I am grateful for:

1. _____

2. _____

3. _____

In the box below, draw **"Thank You"**. Allow your creativity and love to flow, and it's okay to doodle. ☺ While you draw, genuinely thank the things you are grateful for.

```
┌────────────────────────────────────────────┐
│                                            │
│                                            │
│                                            │
│                                            │
│                                            │
│                                            │
│                                            │
└────────────────────────────────────────────┘
```

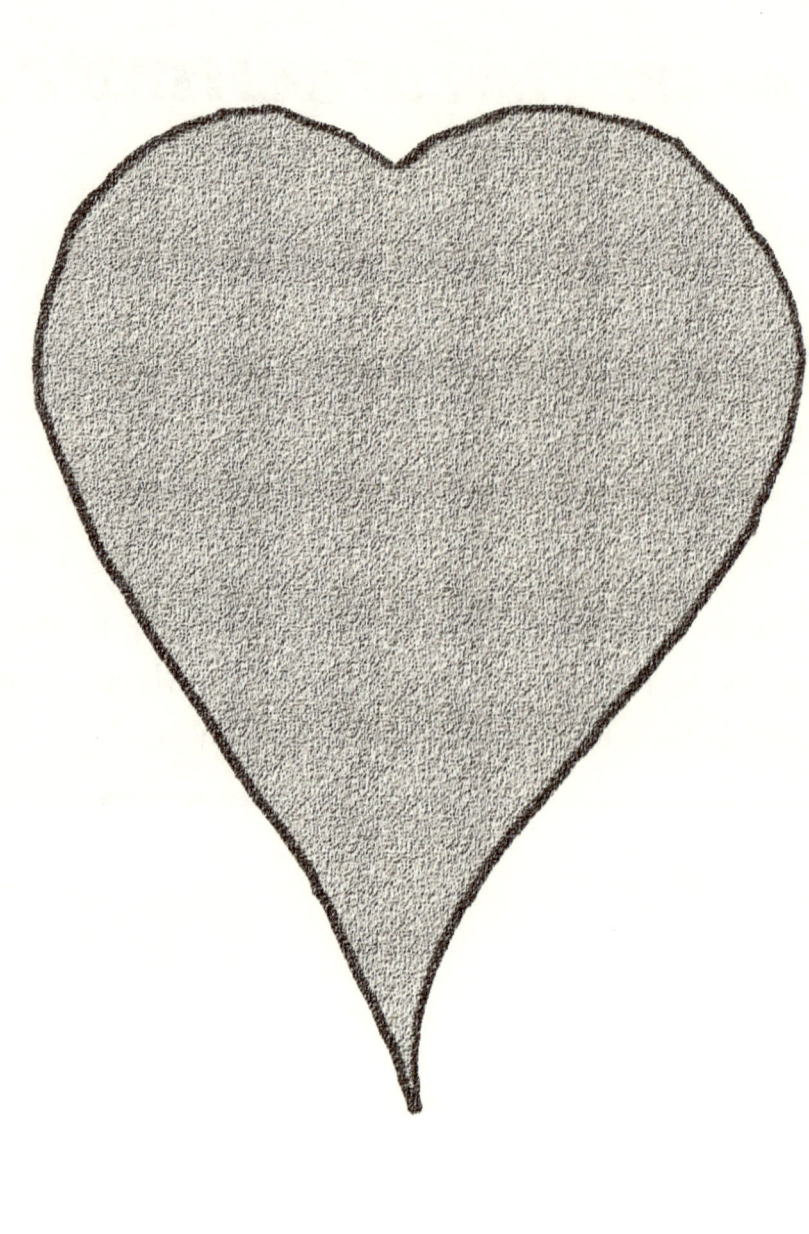

Date: ____/____/____ Day: 9

AN ATTITUDE OF GRATITUDE.

Today, I am grateful for:

1. _____

2. _____

3. _____

In the box below, draw **"Thank You"**. Allow your creativity and love to flow, and it's okay to doodle. ☺ While you draw, genuinely thank the things you are grateful for.

Date: ___/___/___   Day: 10

AN ATTITUDE OF GRATITUDE.

Today, I am grateful for:

1. _____

2. _____

3. _____

In the box below, draw **"Thank You"**. Allow your creativity and love to flow, and it's okay to doodle. ☺ While you draw, genuinely thank the things you are grateful for.

"The unthankful heart discovers no; but the thankful heart will find, in every hour, some heavenly blessings." - **HENRY WARD BEECHER**

Date: ___/___/___   Day: 11

AN ATTITUDE OF GRATITUDE.

Today, I am grateful for:

1. _____

2. _____

3. _____

In the box below, draw **"Thank You"**. Allow your creativity and love to flow, and it's okay to doodle. ☺ While you draw, genuinely thank the things you are grateful for.

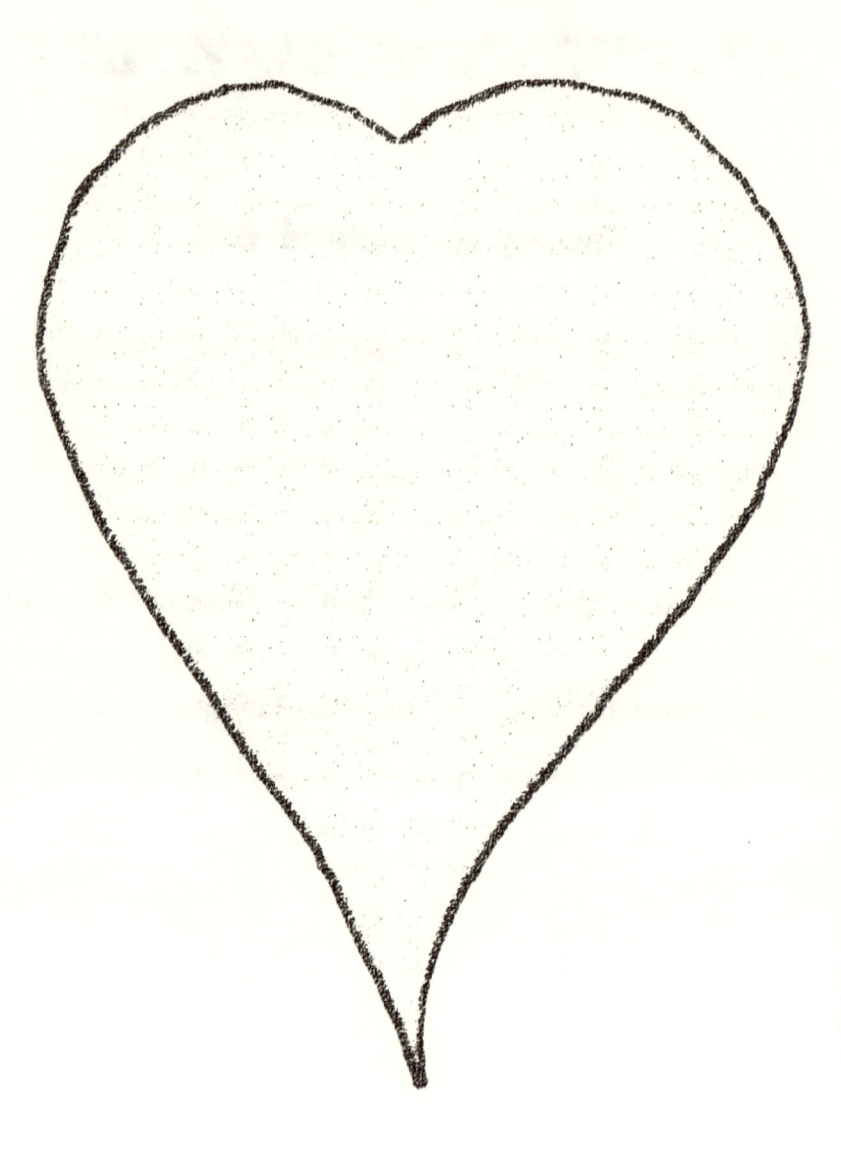

Date: ___/___/___   Day: 12

AN ATTITUDE OF GRATITUDE.

Today, I am grateful for:

1. _____

2. _____

3. _____

In the box below, draw **"Thank You"**. Allow your creativity and love to flow, and it's okay to doodle. ☺ While you draw, genuinely thank the things you are grateful for.

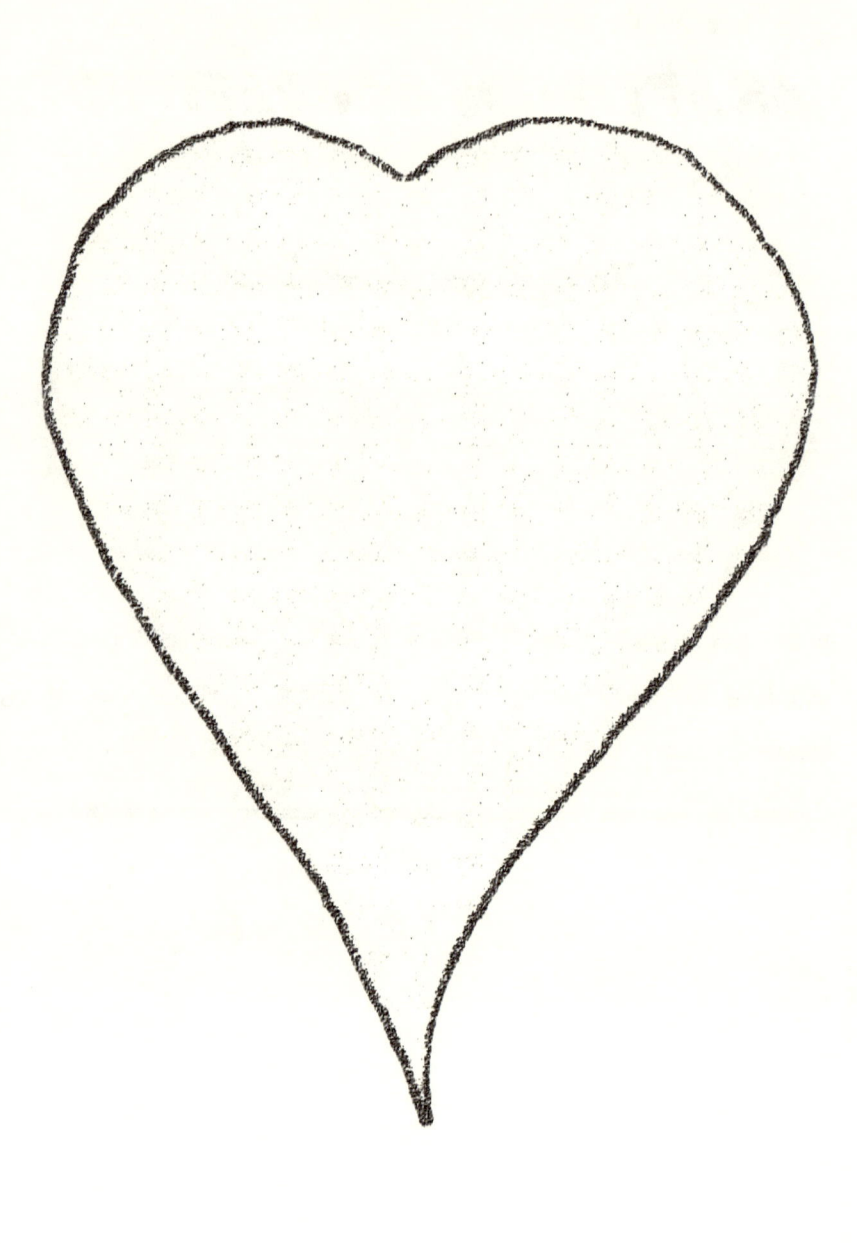

Date: ____/____/____   Day: 13

AN ATTITUDE OF GRATITUDE.

Today, I am grateful for:

1. _____

2. _____

3. _____

In the box below, draw **"Thank You"**. Allow your creativity and love to flow, and it's okay to doodle. ☺ While you draw, genuinely thank the things you are grateful for.

"Gratitude is Riches. Complaint is poverty." - **DORIS DAY**

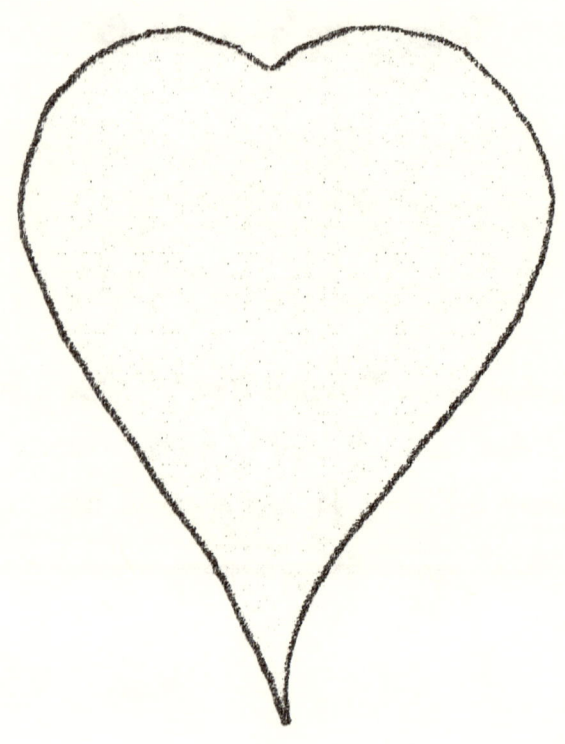

Date: ____/____/____   Day: 14

AN ATTITUDE OF GRATITUDE.

Today, I am grateful for:

1. _____

2. _____

3. _____

In the box below, draw **"Thank You"**. Allow your creativity and love to flow, and it's okay to doodle.☺ While you draw, genuinely thank the things you are grateful for.

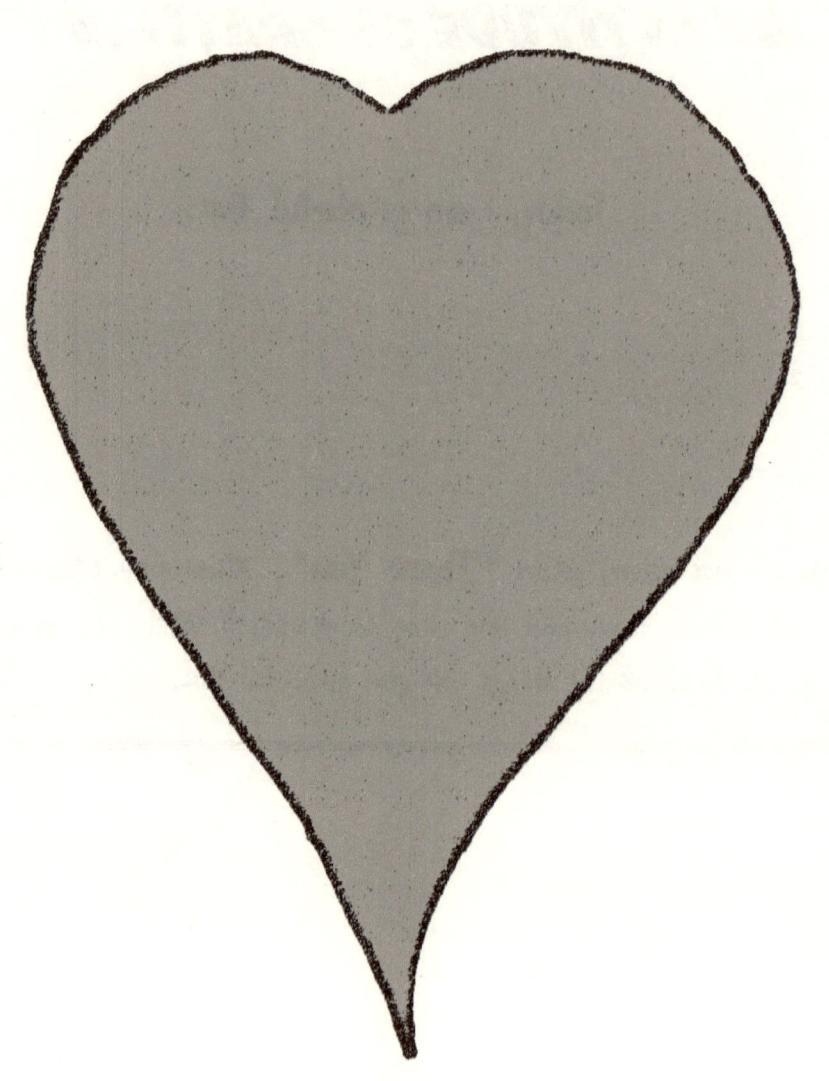

Date: ___/___/___   Day: 15

AN ATTITUDE OF GRATITUDE.

Today, I am grateful for:

1. _____

2. _____

3. _____

In the box below, draw **"Thank You"**. Allow your creativity and love to flow, and it's okay to doodle. ☺ While you draw, genuinely thank the things you are grateful for.

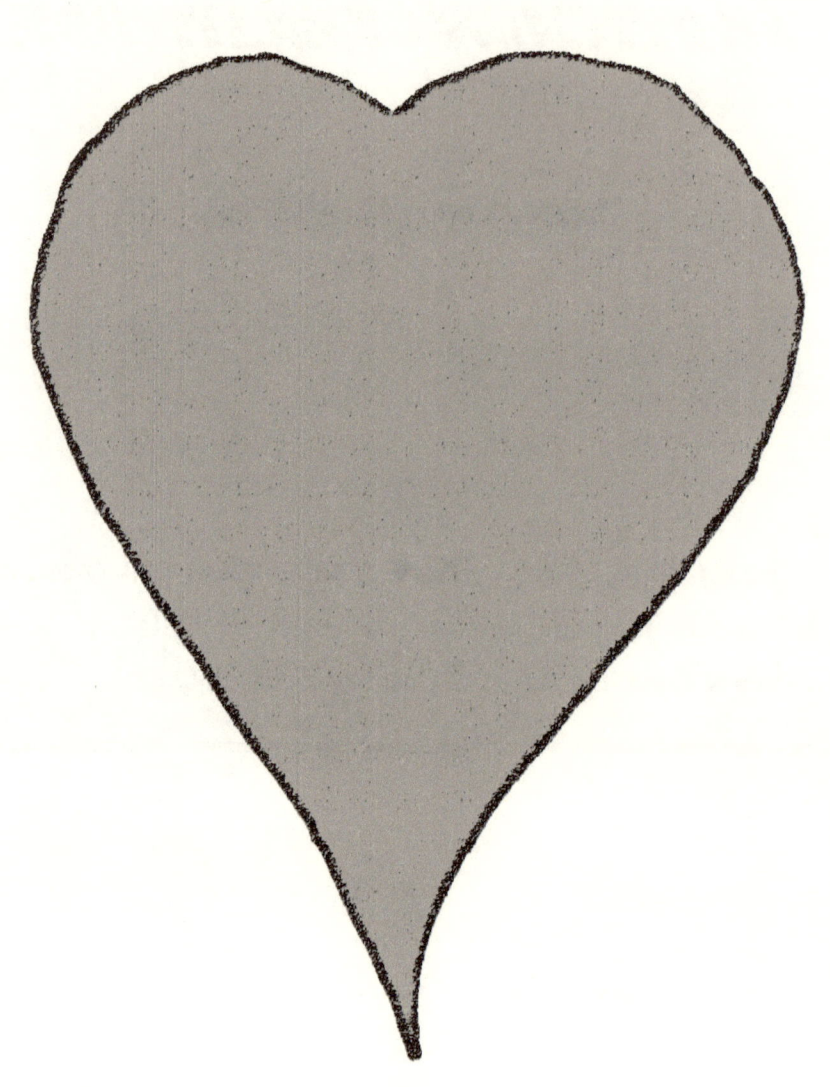

Date: ____/____/____   Day: 16

AN ATTITUDE OF GRATITUDE.

Today, I am grateful for:

1. _____

2. _____

3. _____

In the box below, draw **"Thank You"**. Allow your creativity and love to flow, and it's okay to doodle. ☺ While you draw, genuinely thank the things you are grateful for.

"There is a calmness to a life lived in gratitude, a quiet joy."
- RALPH H. BLUM

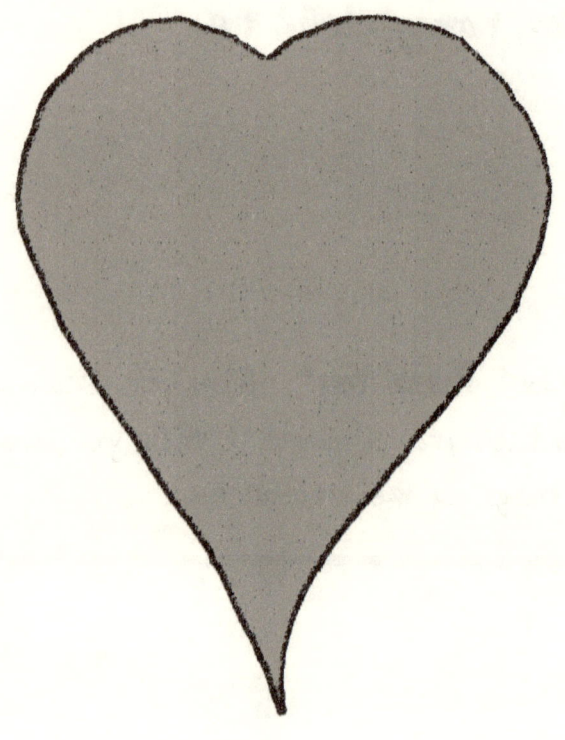

Date: ____/____/____   Day: 17

AN ATTITUDE OF GRATITUDE.

Today, I am grateful for:

1. _____

2. _____

3. _____

In the box below, draw **"Thank You"**. Allow your creativity and love to flow, and it's okay to doodle.☺ While you draw, genuinely thank the things you are grateful for.

Date: ___/___/___   Day: 18

AN ATTITUDE OF GRATITUDE.

Today, I am grateful for:

1. _____

2. _____

3. _____

In the box below, draw **"Thank You"**. Allow your creativity and love to flow, and it's okay to doodle. ☺ While you draw, genuinely thank the things you are grateful for.

Date: ____/____/____   Day: 19

AN ATTITUDE OF GRATITUDE.

Today, I am grateful for:

1. _____
2. _____
3. _____

In the box below, draw **"Thank You"**. Allow your creativity and love to flow, and it's okay to doodle. ☺ While you draw, genuinely thank the things you are grateful for.

"When a person doesn't have gratitude, something is missing in his or her . A person can almost be defined by his or her attitude toward gratitude." - ELIE WIESEL

Date: ____/____/____   Day: 20

AN ATTITUDE OF GRATITUDE.

Today, I am grateful for:

1. _____
2. _____
3. _____

In the box below, draw **"Thank You"**. Allow your creativity and love to flow, and it's okay to doodle.☺ While you draw, genuinely thank the things you are grateful for.

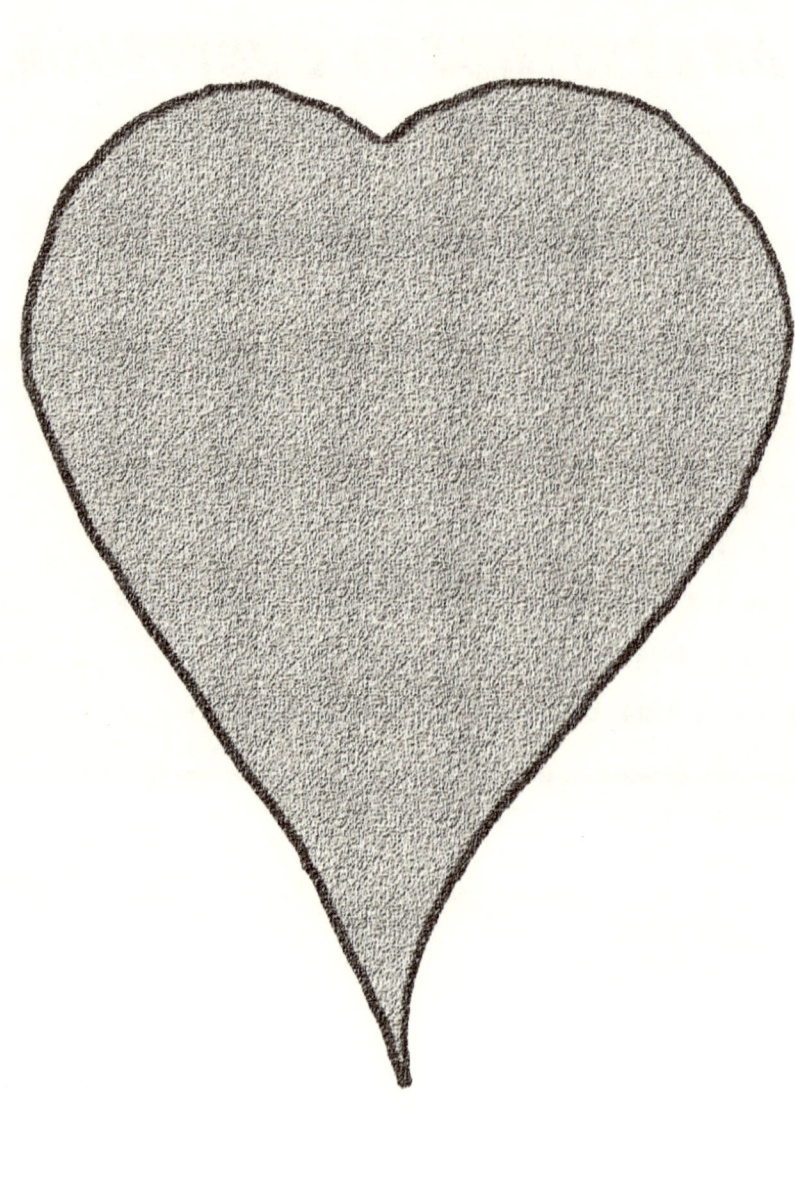

Date: ____/____/____   Day: 21

AN ATTITUDE OF GRATITUDE.

Today, I am grateful for:

1. _____

2. _____

3. _____

In the box below, draw **"Thank You"**. Allow your creativity and love to flow, and it's okay to doodle. ☺ While you draw, genuinely thank the things you are grateful for.

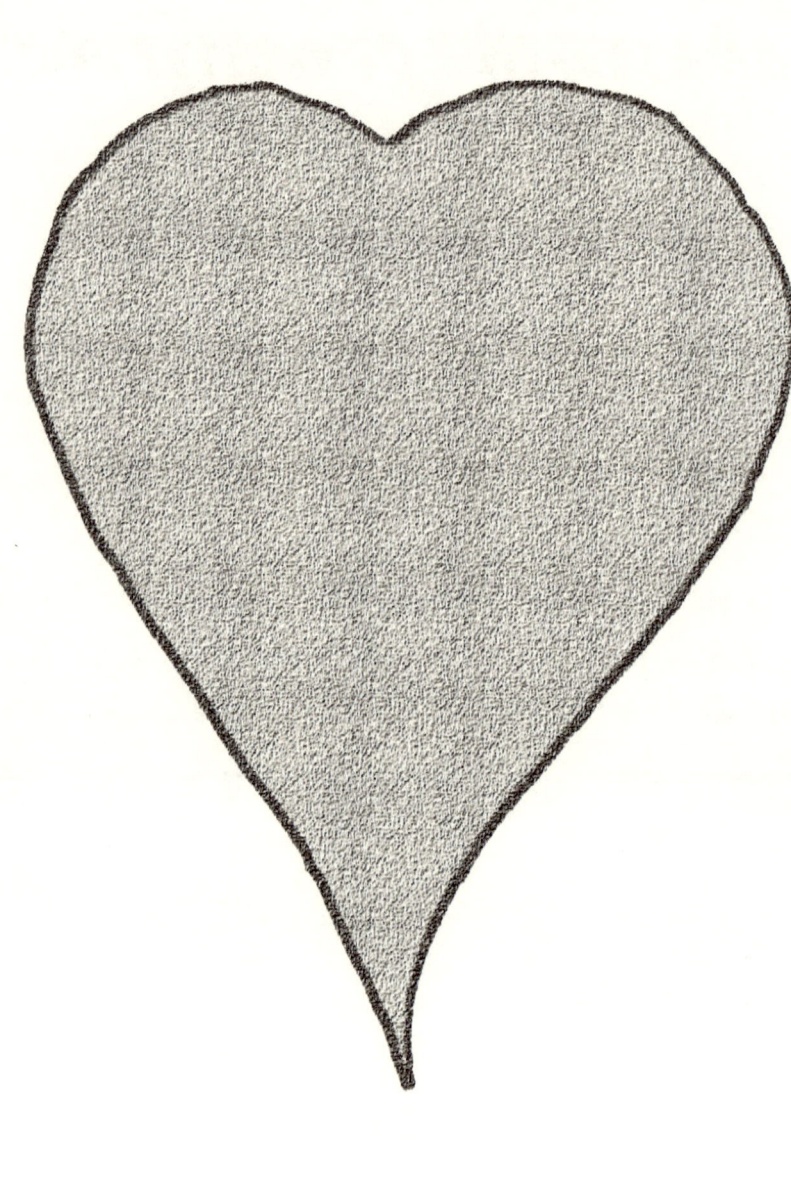

Date: ____/____/____   Day: 22

AN ATTITUDE OF GRATITUDE.

Today, I am grateful for:

1. _____

2. _____

3. _____

In the box below, draw **"Thank You"**. Allow your creativity and love to flow, and it's okay to doodle. ☺ While you draw, genuinely thank the things you are grateful for.

"Let gratitude be the pillow upon which you kneel to say your nightly prayer." - MAYA ANGELOU

Date: ___/___/___ Day: 23

AN ATTITUDE OF GRATITUDE.

Today, I am grateful for:

1. _____

2. _____

3. _____

In the box below, draw **"Thank You"**. Allow your creativity and love to flow, and it's okay to doodle. ☺ While you draw, genuinely thank the things you are grateful for.

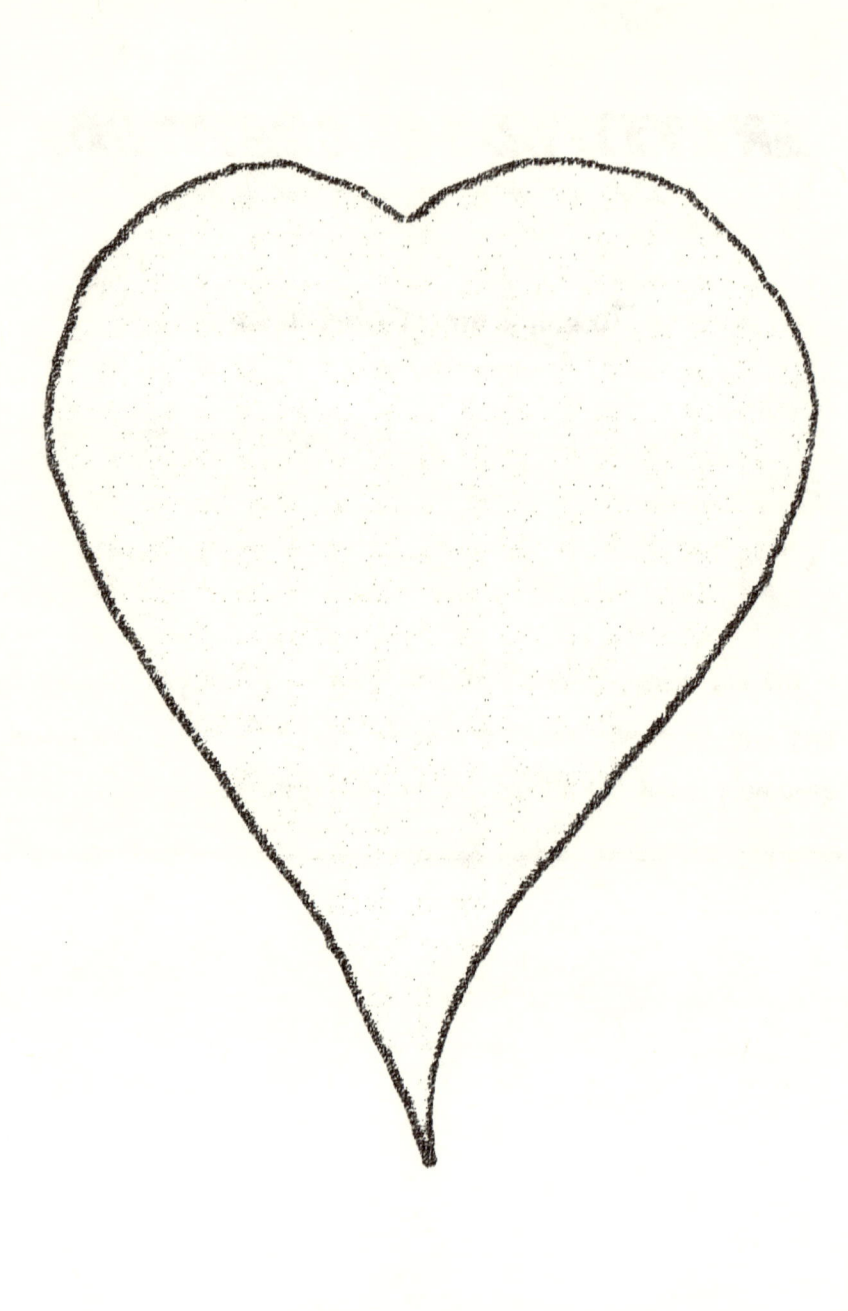

Date: ____/____/____   Day: 24

AN ATTITUDE OF GRATITUDE.

Today, I am grateful for:

1. _____
2. _____
3. _____

In the box below, draw **"Thank You"**. Allow your creativity and love to flow, and it's okay to doodle. ☺ While you draw, genuinely thank the things you are grateful for.

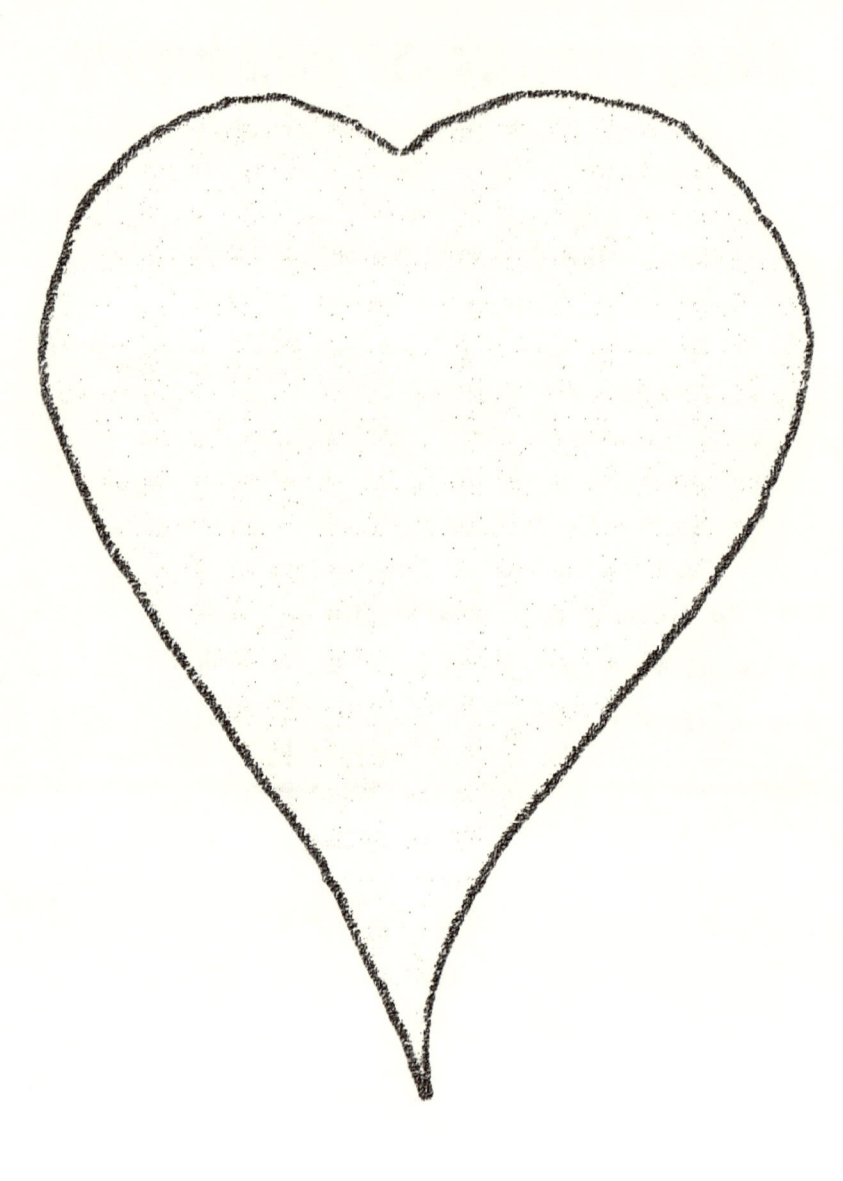

Date: ____/____/____   Day: 25

AN ATTITUDE OF GRATITUDE.

Today, I am grateful for:

1. _____

2. _____

3. _____

In the box below, draw **"Thank You"**. Allow your creativity and love to flow, and it's okay to doodle.☺ While you draw, genuinely thank the things you are grateful for.

"I am happy because I'm grateful. I choose to be grateful." - **WILL ARNETT**

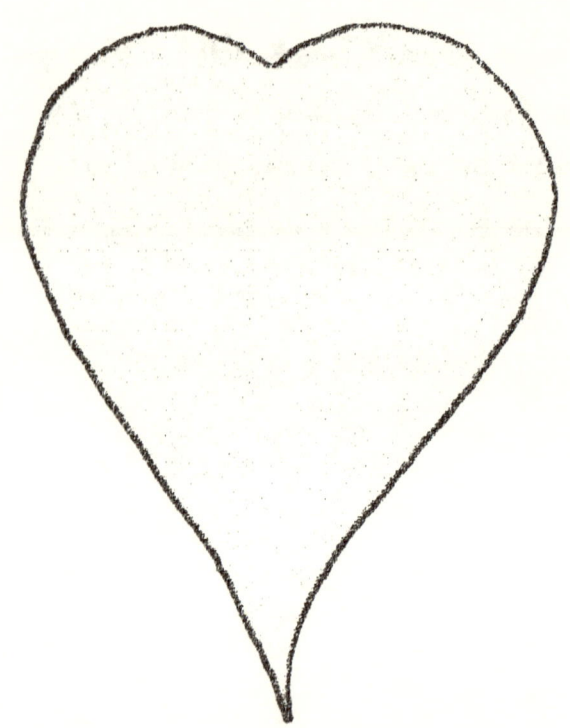

Date: ____/____/____ Day: 26

AN ATTITUDE OF GRATITUDE.

Today, I am grateful for:

1. _____

2. _____

3. _____

In the box below, draw **"Thank You"**. Allow your creativity and love to flow, and it's okay to doodle. ☺ While you draw, genuinely thank the things you are grateful for.

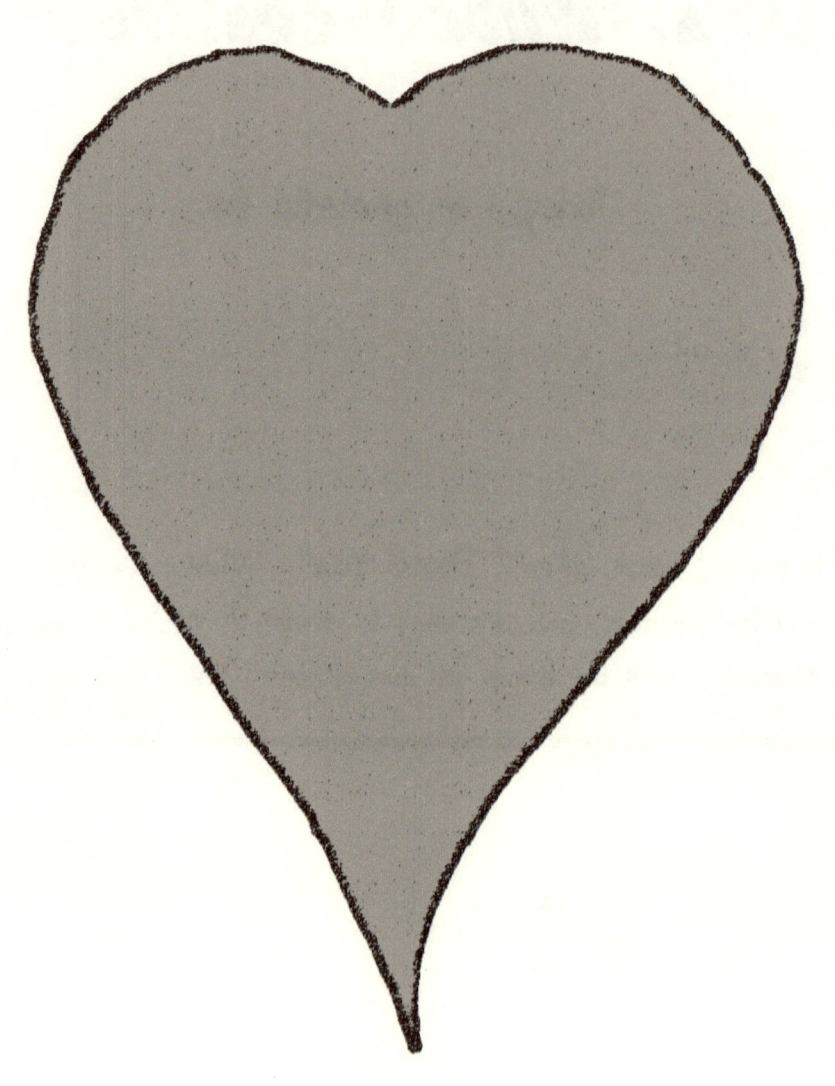

Date: ____/____/____   Day: 27

AN ATTITUDE OF GRATITUDE.

Today, I am grateful for:

1. _____

2. _____

3. _____

In the box below, draw **"Thank You"**. Allow your creativity and love to flow, and it's okay to doodle. ☺ While you draw, genuinely thank the things you are grateful for.

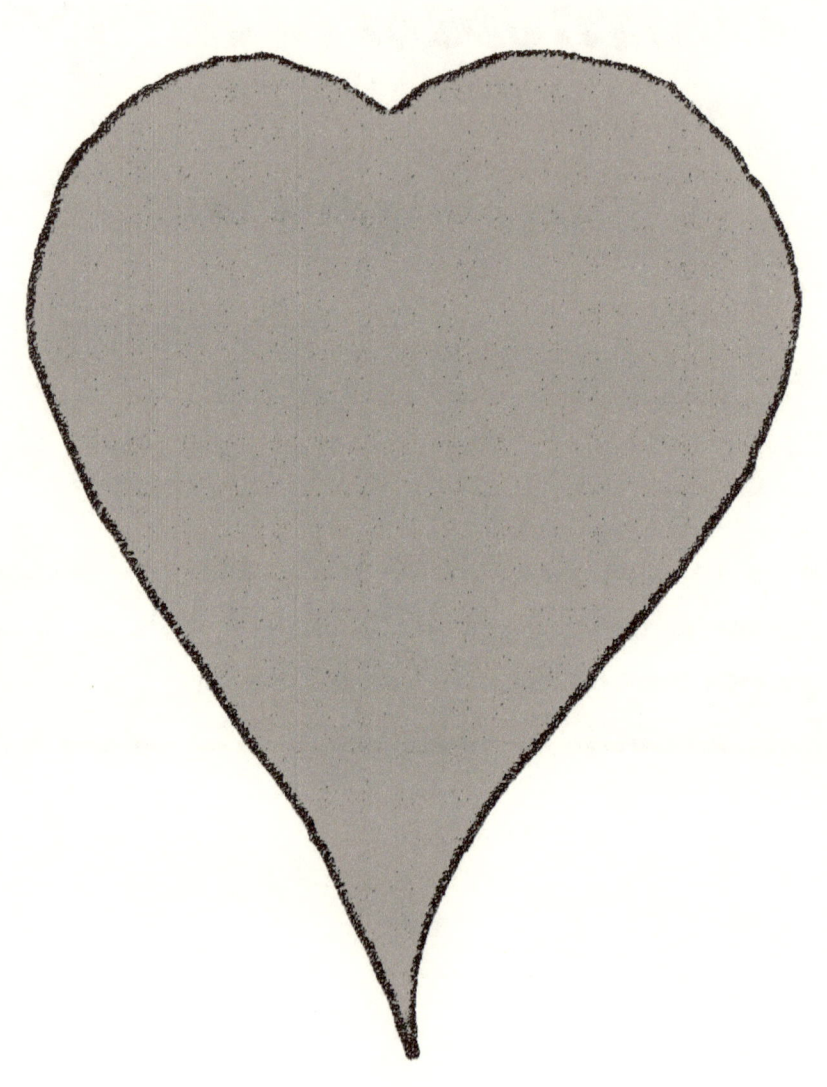

Date: ____/____/____   Day: 28

AN ATTITUDE OF GRATITUDE.

Today, I am grateful for:

1. _____
2. _____
3. _____

In the box below, draw **"Thank You"**. Allow your creativity and love to flow, and it's okay to doodle. ☺ While you draw, genuinely thank the things you are grateful for.

"Gratitude, warm, sincere, intense, when it takes of the bosom, fills the soul to overflowing and scarce leaves room for any other sentiment or thought." - **JOHN QUINCY ADAMS**

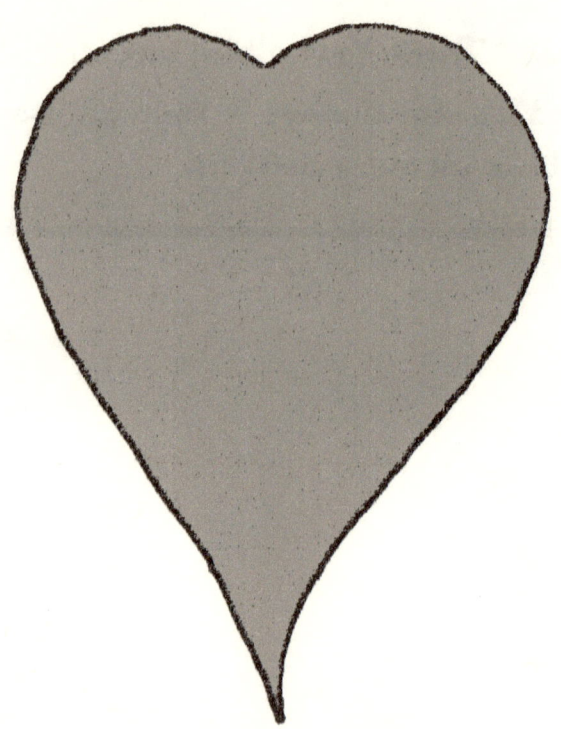

Date: ____/____/____　　　　　　　　　　　　　Day: 29

AN ATTITUDE OF GRATITUDE.

Today, I am grateful for:

1. _____

2. _____

3. _____

In the box below, draw **"Thank You"**. Allow your creativity and love to flow, and it's okay to doodle. ☺ While you draw, genuinely thank the things you are grateful for.

Date: ___/___/___   Day: 30

AN ATTITUDE OF GRATITUDE.

Today, I am grateful for:

1. _____

2. _____

3. _____

In the box below, draw **"Thank You"**. Allow your creativity and love to flow, and it's okay to doodle.☺ While you draw, genuinely thank the things you are grateful for.

Date: ____/____/____ Day: 31

AN ATTITUDE OF GRATITUDE.

Today, I am grateful for:

1. _____
2. _____
3. _____

In the box below, draw **"Thank You"**. Allow your creativity and love to flow, and it's okay to doodle. ☺ While you draw, genuinely thank the things you are grateful for.

"When we focus on our gratitude, the tide of disappointment goes out and the tide of love rushes in." - **KRISTIN ARMSTRONG**

Date: ___/___/___ Day: 32

AN ATTITUDE OF GRATITUDE.

Today, I am grateful for:

1. _____

2. _____

3. _____

In the box below, draw **"Thank You"**. Allow your creativity and love to flow, and it's okay to doodle. ☺ While you draw, genuinely thank the things you are grateful for.

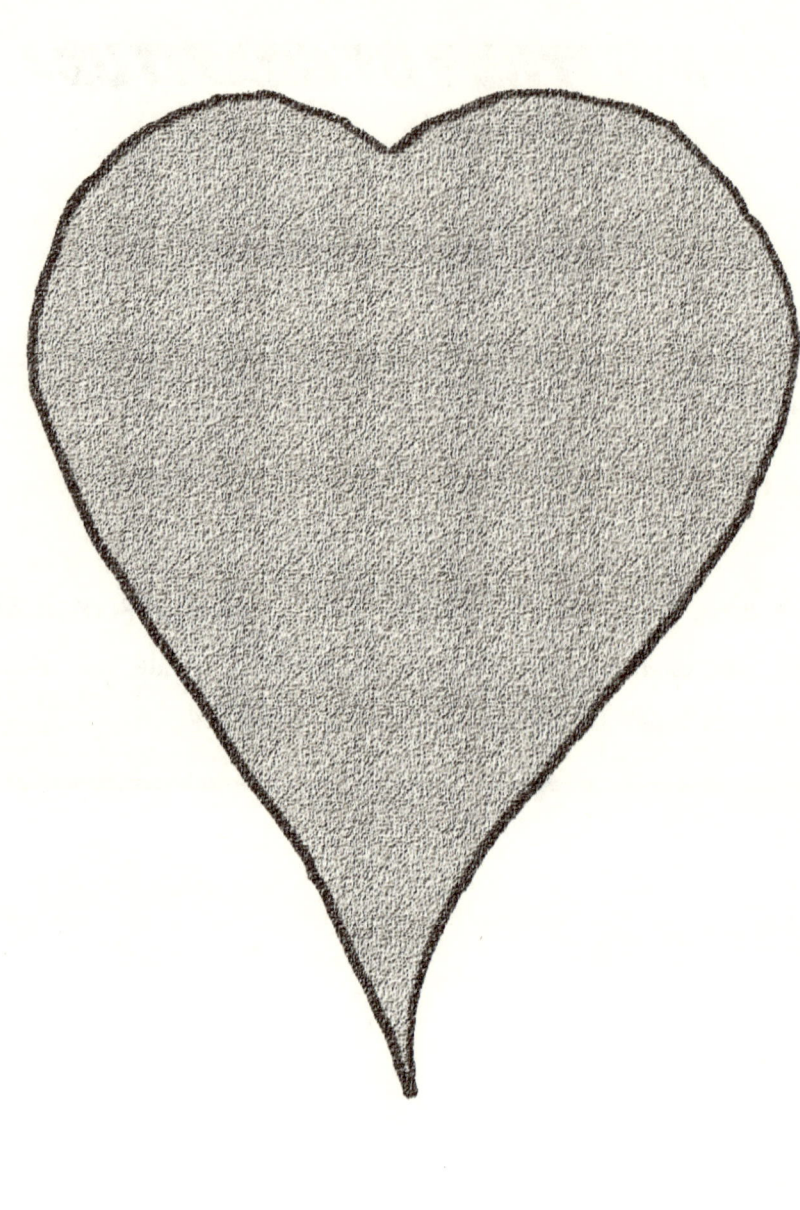

Date: ___/___/___   Day: 33

AN ATTITUDE OF GRATITUDE.

Today, I am grateful for:

1. _____

2. _____

3. _____

In the box below, draw **"Thank You"**. Allow your creativity and love to flow, and it's okay to doodle. ☺ While you draw, genuinely thank the things you are grateful for.

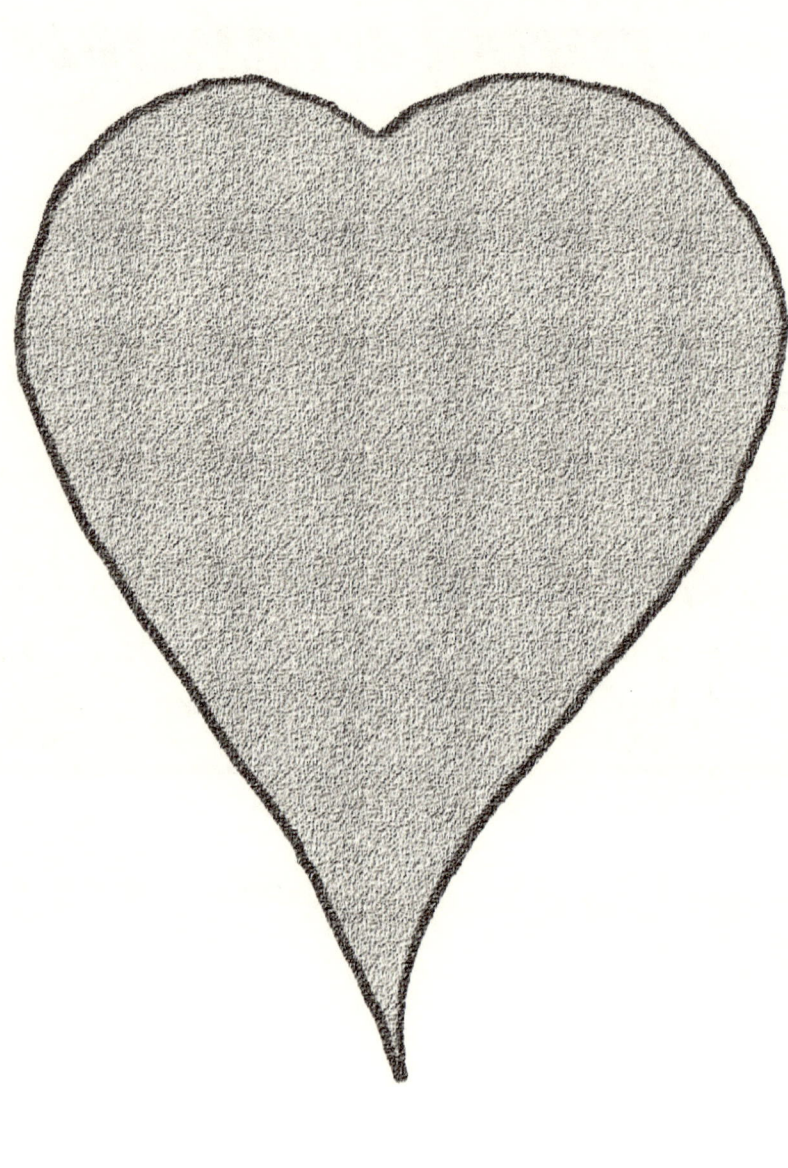

Date: ____/____/____   Day: 34

AN ATTITUDE OF GRATITUDE.

Today, I am grateful for:

1. _____

2. _____

3. _____

In the box below, draw **"Thank You"**. Allow your creativity and love to flow, and it's okay to doodle. ☺ While you draw, genuinely thank the things you are grateful for.

"No one who achieves success does so without the help of others. The wise and confident acknowledge this help with gratitude." -
ALFRED NORTH WHITEHEAD

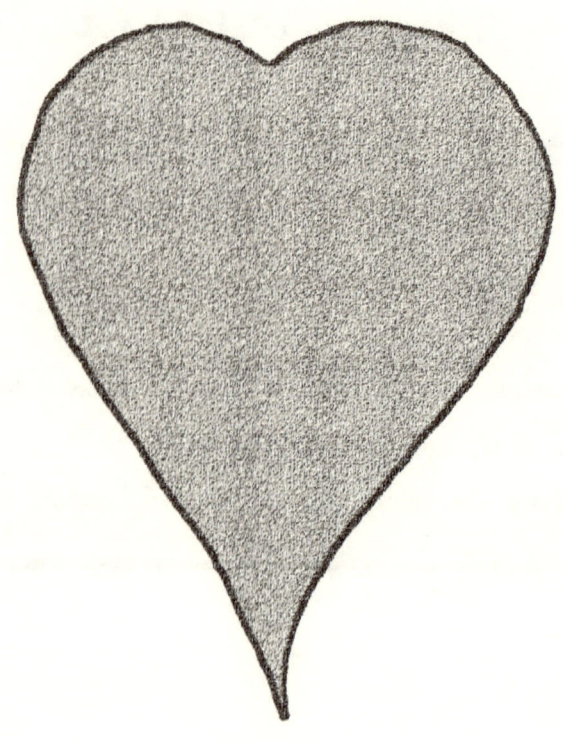

Date: ___/___/___   Day: 35

AN ATTITUDE OF GRATITUDE.

Today, I am grateful for:

1. _____

2. _____

3. _____

In the box below, draw **"Thank You"**. Allow your creativity and love to flow, and it's okay to doodle. ☺ While you draw, genuinely thank the things you are grateful for.

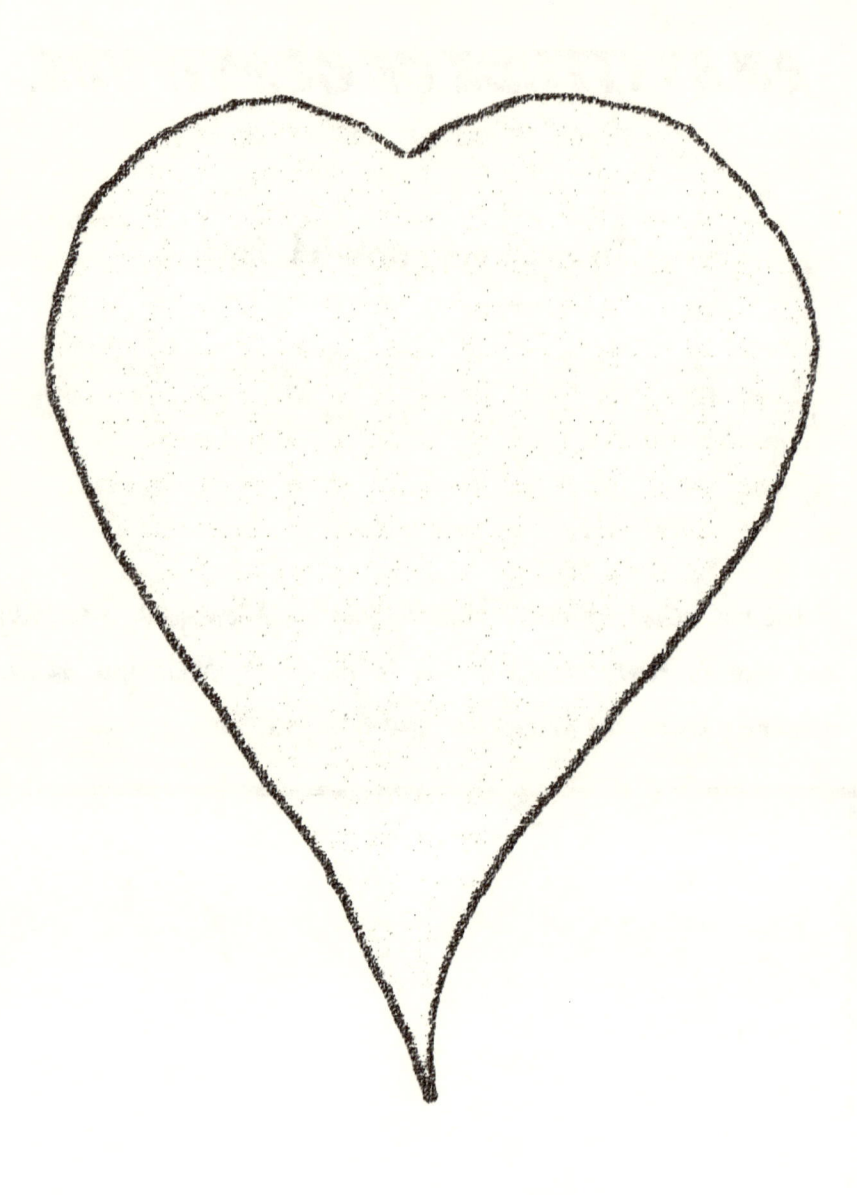

Date: ___/___/___   Day: 36

AN ATTITUDE OF GRATITUDE.

Today, I am grateful for:

1. _____

2. _____

3. _____

In the box below, draw **"Thank You"**. Allow your creativity and love to flow, and it's okay to doodle. ☺ While you draw, genuinely thank the things you are grateful for.

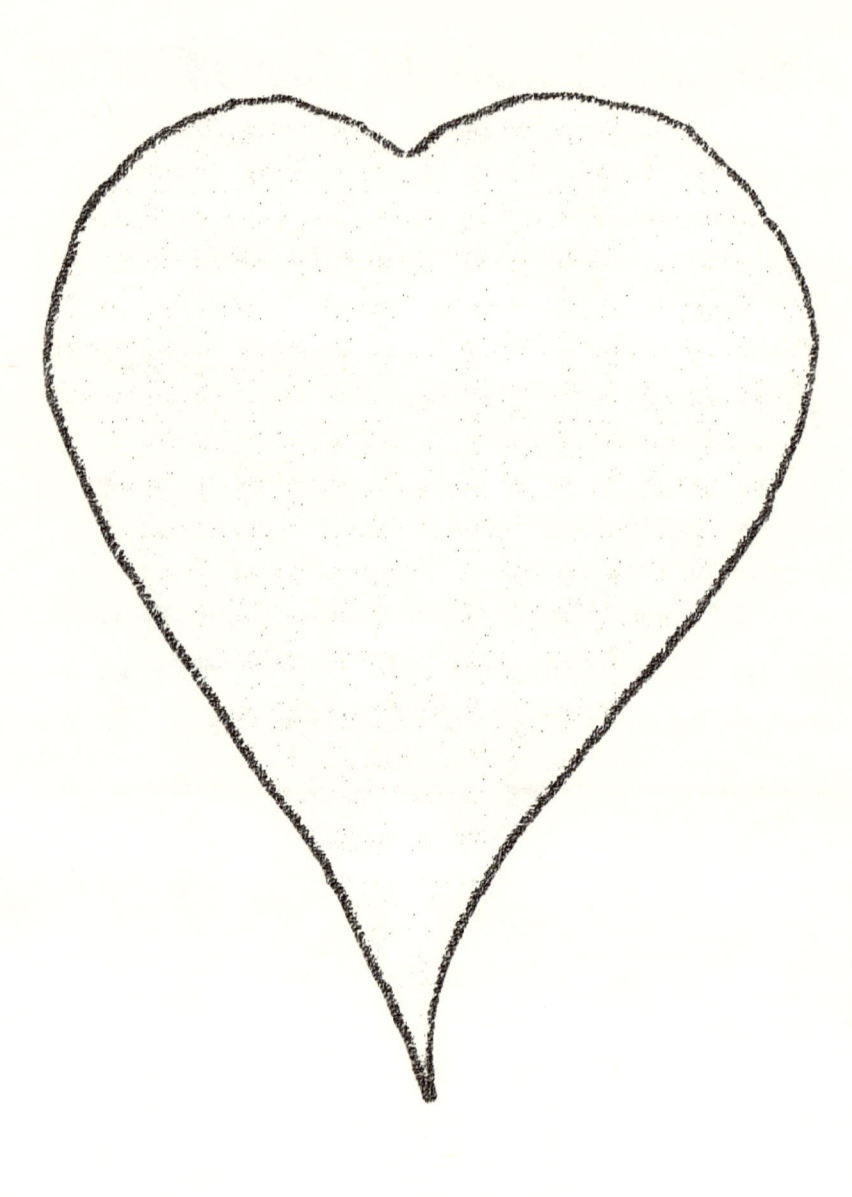

Date: ____/____/____　　　　　　　　　　　　　　　Day: 37

AN ATTITUDE OF GRATITUDE.

Today, I am grateful for:

1. _____

2. _____

3. _____

In the box below, draw **"Thank You"**. Allow your creativity and love to flow, and it's okay to doodle. ☺ While you draw, genuinely thank the things you are grateful for.

"Gratitude unlocks all that's blocking us from really feeling truthful, really feeling authentic and vulnerable and happy." - **GABRIELLE BERNSTEIN**

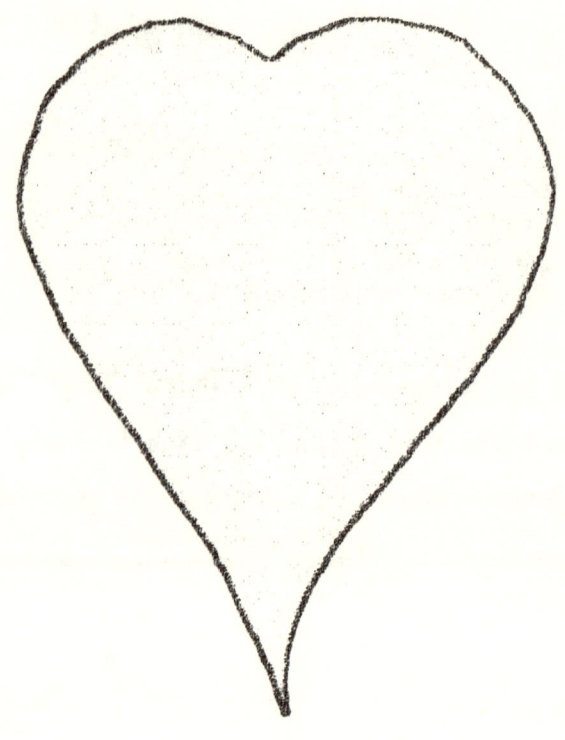

Date: ___/___/___   Day: 38

AN ATTITUDE OF GRATITUDE.

Today, I am grateful for:

1. _____

2. _____

3. _____

In the box below, draw **"Thank You"**. Allow your creativity and love to flow, and it's okay to doodle. ☺ While you draw, genuinely thank the things you are grateful for.

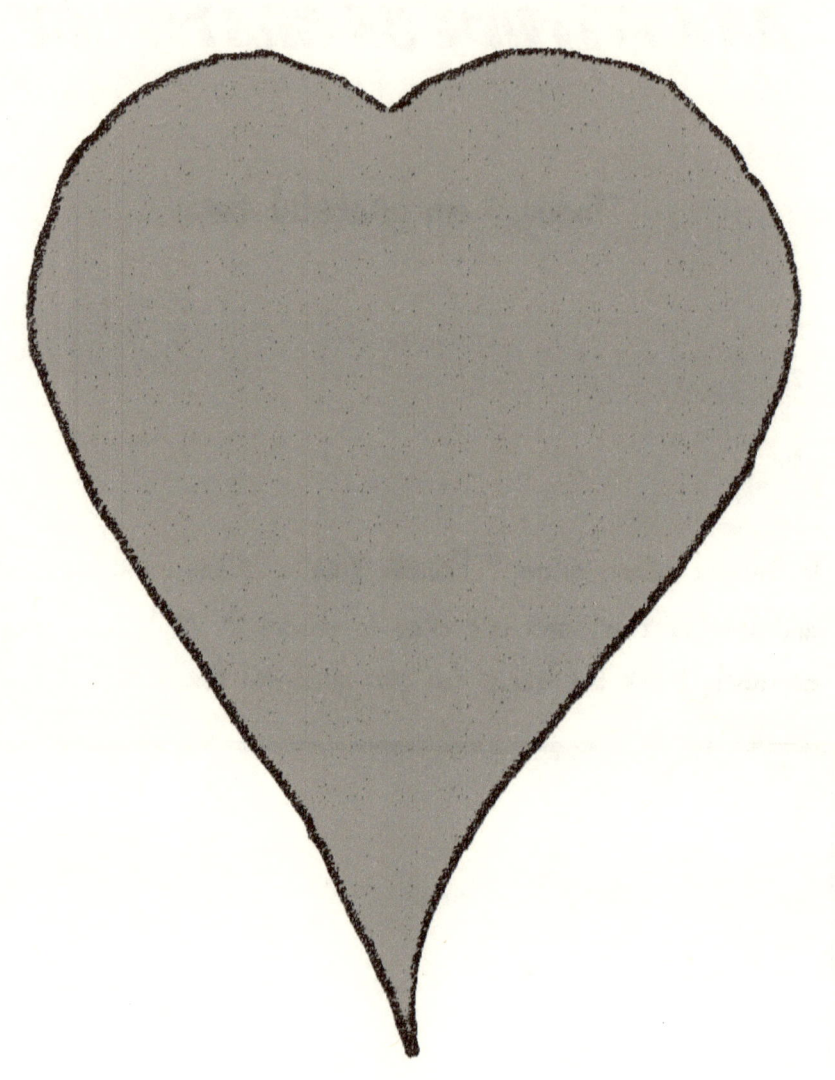

Date: ____/____/____   Day: 39

AN ATTITUDE OF GRATITUDE.

Today, I am grateful for:

1. _____
2. _____
3. _____

In the box below, draw **"Thank You"**. Allow your creativity and love to flow, and it's okay to doodle.☺ While you draw, genuinely thank the things you are grateful for.

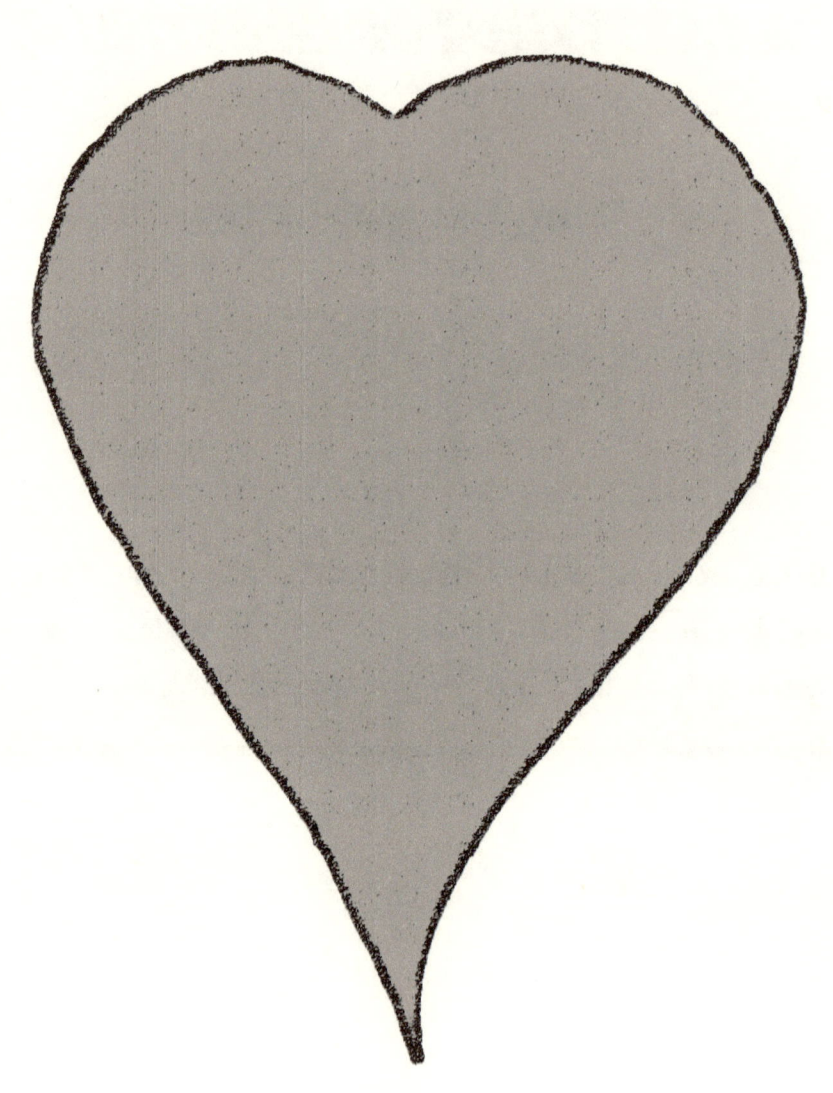

Date: ____/____/____   Day: 40

AN ATTITUDE OF GRATITUDE.

Today, I am grateful for:

1. _____

2. _____

3. _____

In the box below, draw **"Thank You"**. Allow your creativity and love to flow, and it's okay to doodle. ☺ While you draw, genuinely thank the things you are grateful for.

"The struggle ends when gratitude begins." - **NEALE DONALD WALSCH**

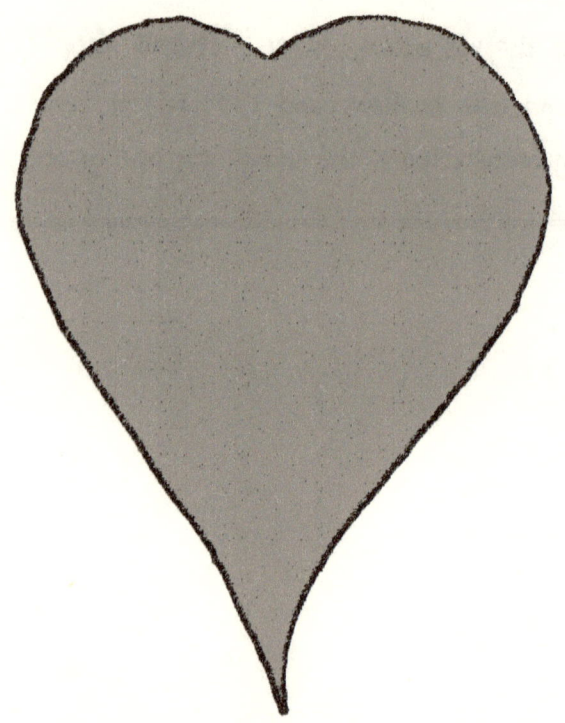

Date: ____/____/____   Day: 41

AN ATTITUDE OF GRATITUDE.

Today, I am grateful for:

1. _____

2. _____

3. _____

In the box below, draw **"Thank You"**. Allow your creativity and love to flow, and it's okay to doodle. ☺ While you draw, genuinely thank the things you are grateful for.

Date: ___/___/___   Day: 42

AN ATTITUDE OF GRATITUDE.

Today, I am grateful for:

1. _____
2. _____
3. _____

In the box below, draw **"Thank You"**. Allow your creativity and love to flow, and it's okay to doodle.☺ While you draw, genuinely thank the things you are grateful for.

Date: ____/____/____   Day: 43

AN ATTITUDE OF GRATITUDE.

Today, I am grateful for:

1. _____
2. _____
3. _____

In the box below, draw **"Thank You"**. Allow your creativity and love to flow, and it's okay to doodle.☺ While you draw, genuinely thank the things you are grateful for.

"If you want to turn your life around, try thankfulness. It will change your life mightily." - GERALD GOOD

Date: ___/___/___   Day: 44

AN ATTITUDE OF GRATITUDE.

Today, I am grateful for:

1. _____
2. _____
3. _____

In the box below, draw **"Thank You"**. Allow your creativity and love to flow, and it's okay to doodle. ☺ While you draw, genuinely thank the things you are grateful for.

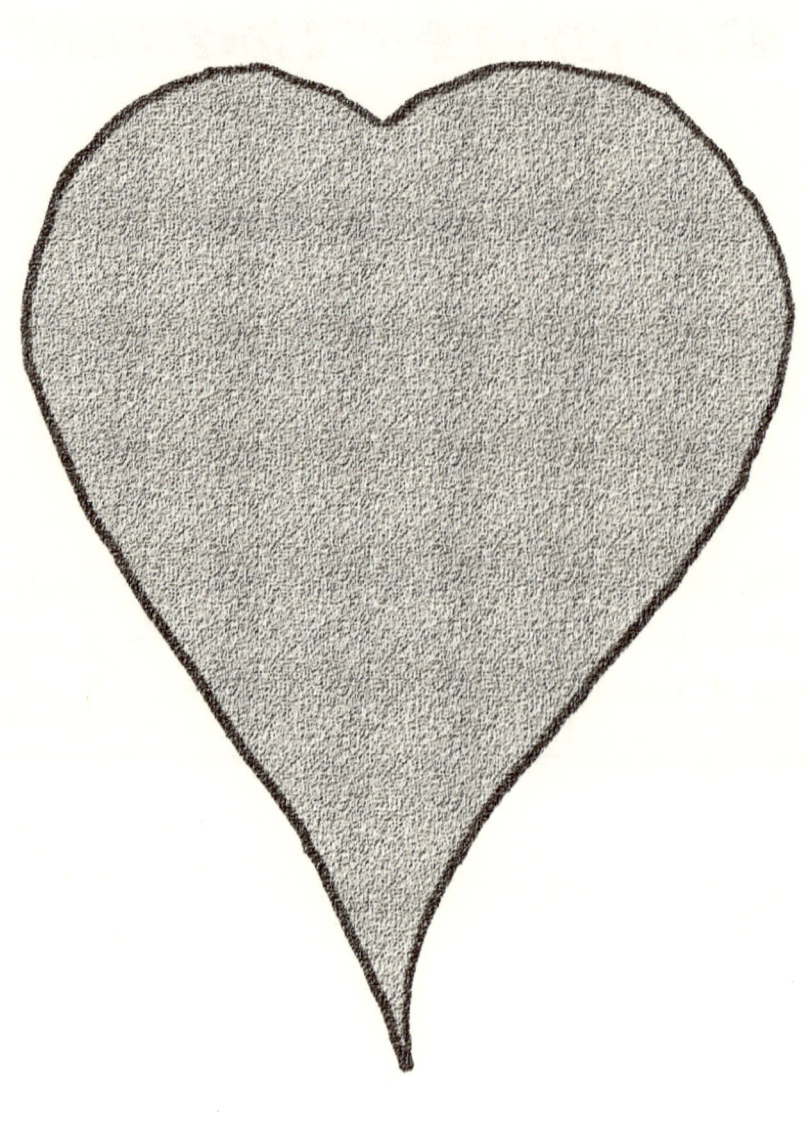

Date: ____/____/____   Day: 45

AN ATTITUDE OF GRATITUDE.

Today, I am grateful for:

1. _____

2. _____

3. _____

In the box below, draw **"Thank You"**. Allow your creativity and love to flow, and it's okay to doodle. ☺ While you draw, genuinely thank the things you are grateful for.

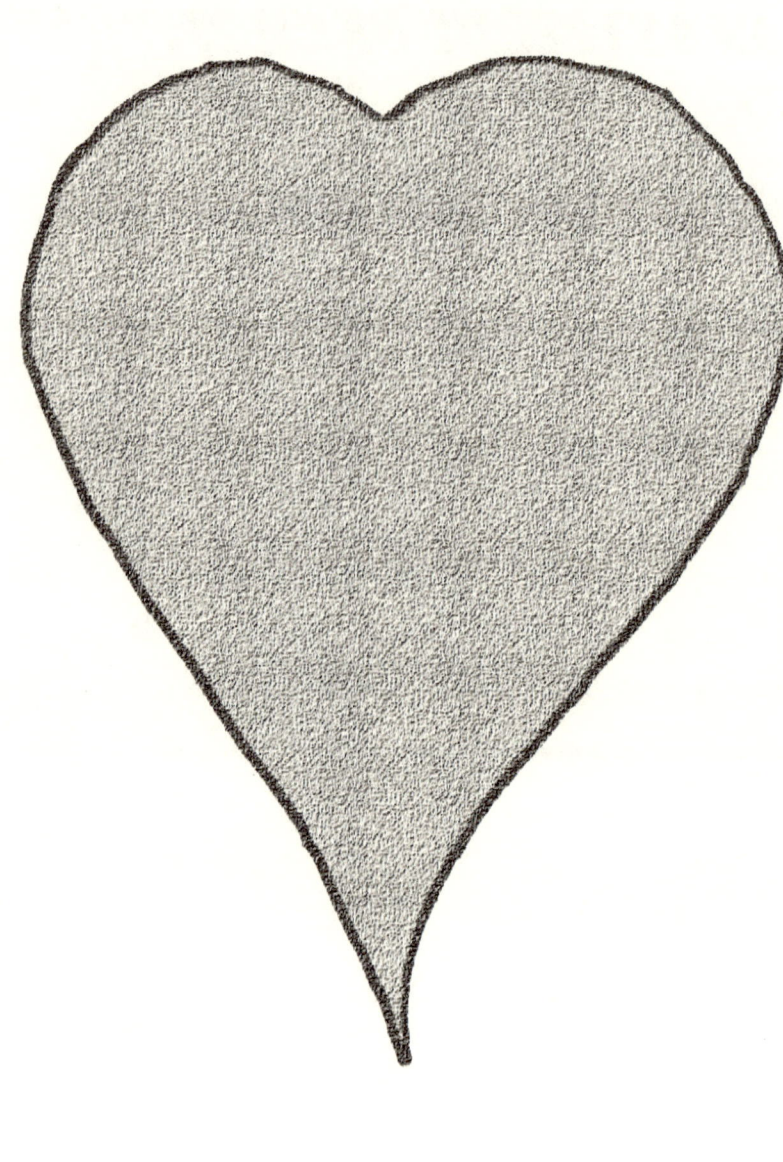

Date: ____/____/____   Day: 46

AN ATTITUDE OF GRATITUDE.

Today, I am grateful for:

1. _____

2. _____

3. _____

In the box below, draw **"Thank You"**. Allow your creativity and love to flow, and it's okay to doodle. ☺ While you draw, genuinely thank the things you are grateful for.

"Find the good and praise it." - **ALEX HALEY**

Date: ____/____/____   Day: 47

AN ATTITUDE OF GRATITUDE.

Today, I am grateful for:

1. _____

2. _____

3. _____

In the box below, draw **"Thank You"**. Allow your creativity and love to flow, and it's okay to doodle.☺ While you draw, genuinely thank the things you are grateful for.

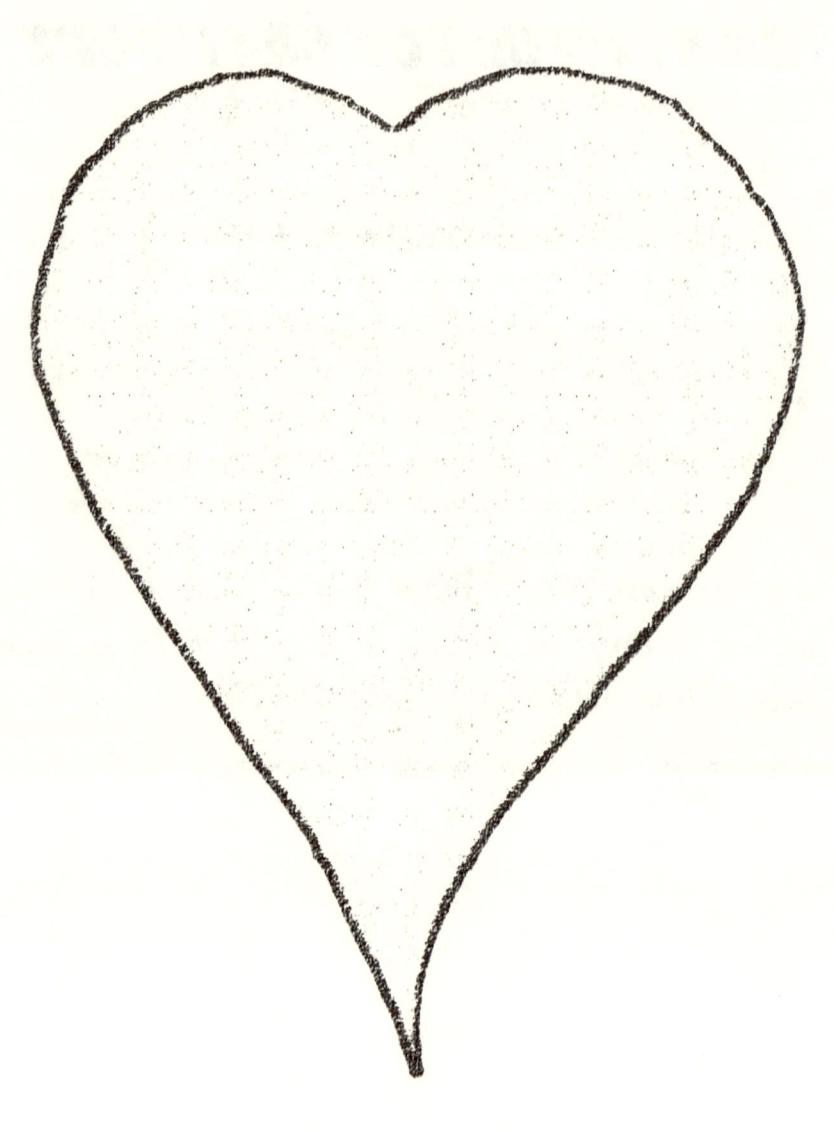

Date: ____/____/____   Day: 48

AN ATTITUDE OF GRATITUDE.

Today, I am grateful for:

1. _____

2. _____

3. _____

In the box below, draw **"Thank You"**. Allow your creativity and love to flow, and it's okay to doodle. ☺ While you draw, genuinely thank the things you are grateful for.

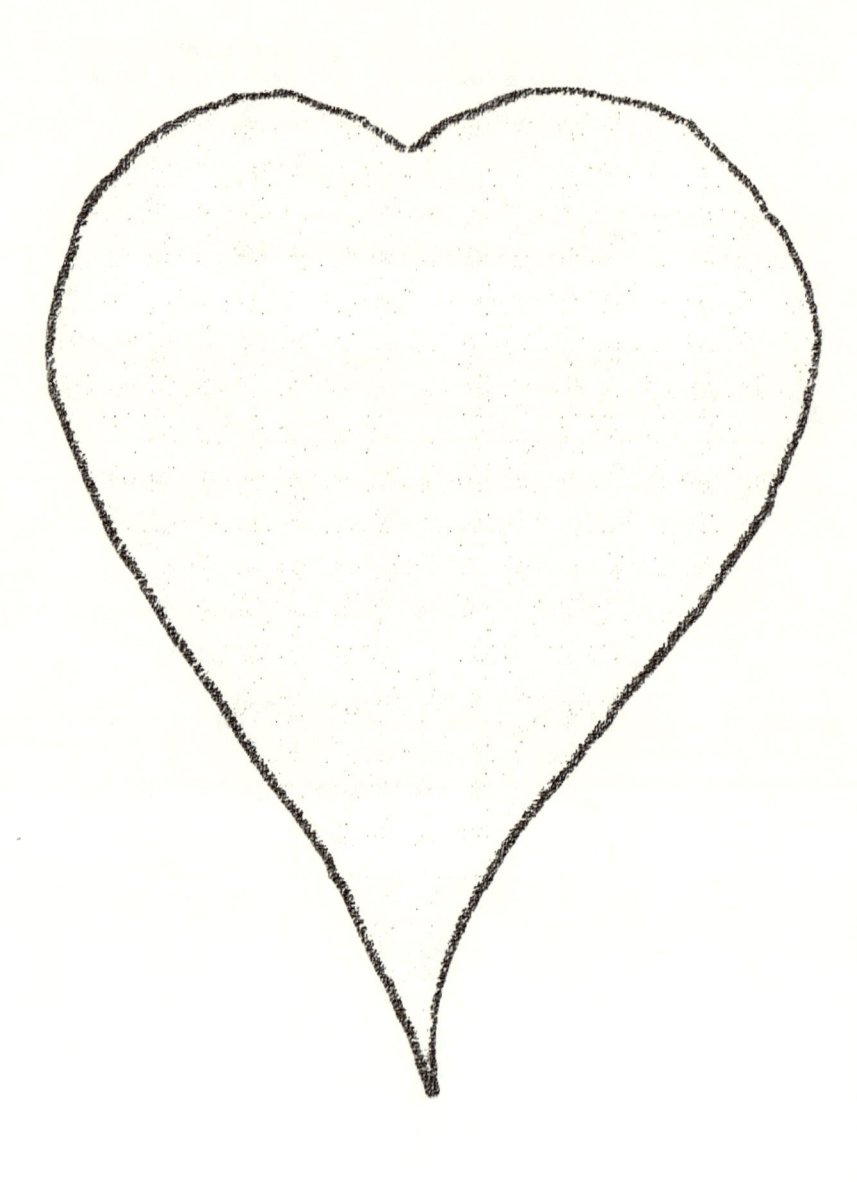

Date: ____/____/____   Day: 49

AN ATTITUDE OF GRATITUDE.

Today, I am grateful for:

1. _____

2. _____

3. _____

In the box below, draw **"Thank You"**. Allow your creativity and love to flow, and it's okay to doodle. ☺ While you draw, genuinely thank the things you are grateful for.

"Gratitude is a currency that we can mint for ourselves, and spend without fear of bankruptcy." - **FRED DE WITT VAN AMBURGH**

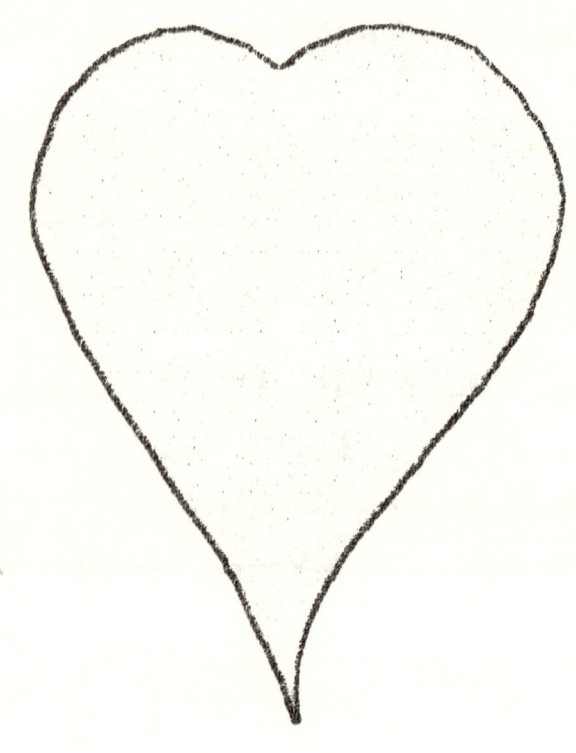

Date: ____/____/____   Day: 50

AN ATTITUDE OF GRATITUDE.

Today, I am grateful for:

1. _____

2. _____

3. _____

In the box below, draw **"Thank You"**. Allow your creativity and love to flow, and it's okay to doodle. ☺ While you draw, genuinely thank the things you are grateful for.

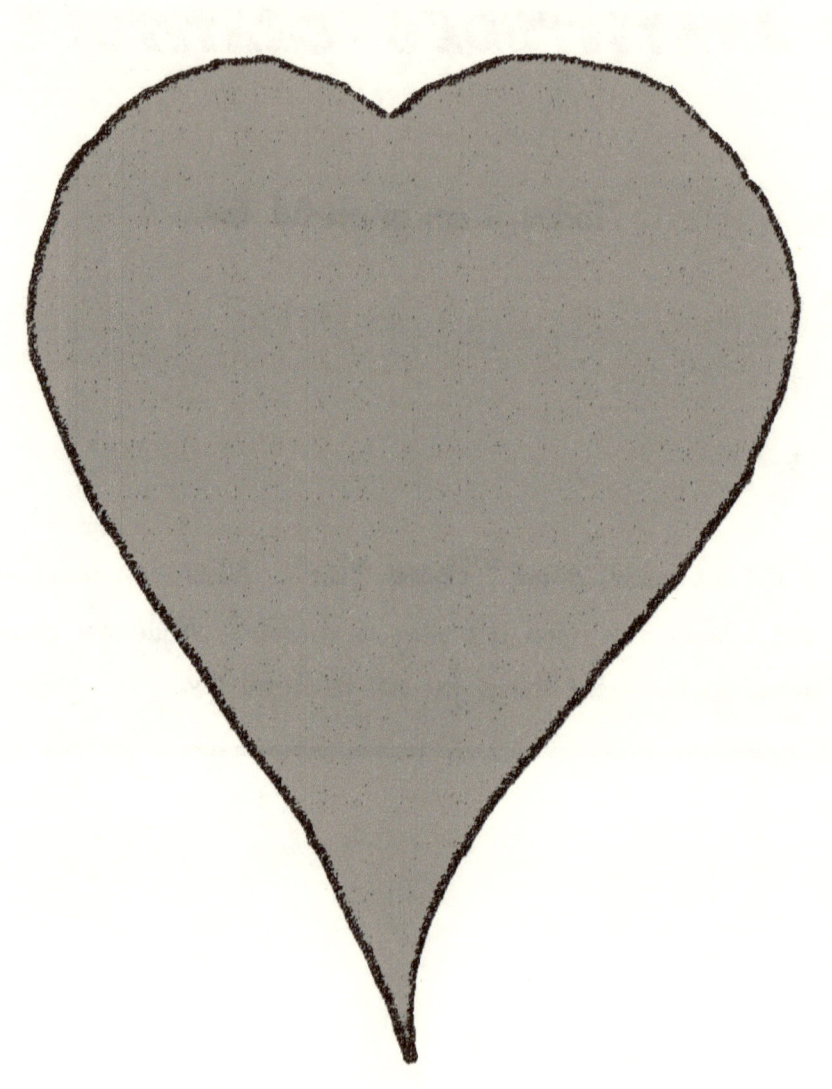

Date: ___/___/___ Day: 51

AN ATTITUDE OF GRATITUDE.

Today, I am grateful for:

1. _____
2. _____
3. _____

In the box below, draw **"Thank You"**. Allow your creativity and love to flow, and it's okay to doodle. ☺ While you draw, genuinely thank the things you are grateful for.

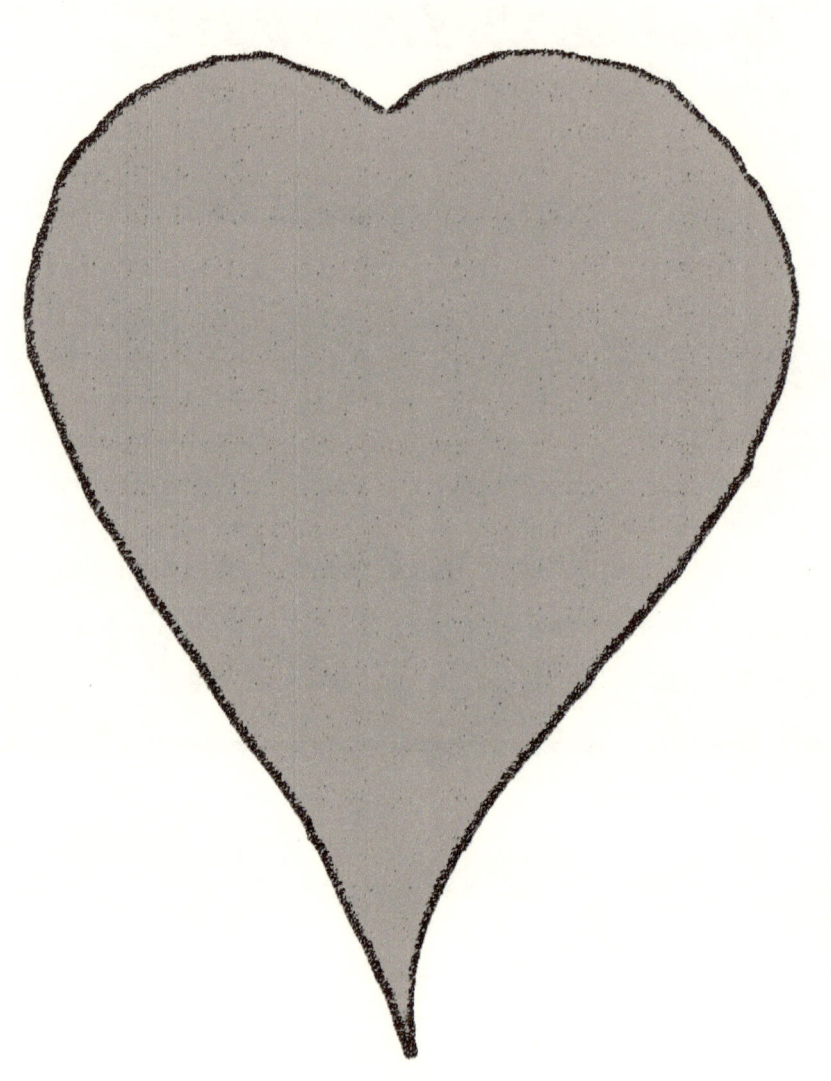

Date: ____/____/____   Day: 52

AN ATTITUDE OF GRATITUDE.

Today, I am grateful for:

1. _____
2. _____
3. _____

In the box below, draw **"Thank You"**. Allow your creativity and love to flow, and it's okay to doodle. ☺ While you draw, genuinely thank the things you are grateful for.

"It is through gratitude for the present moment that the spiritual dimension of life opens up." - ECKHART TOLLE

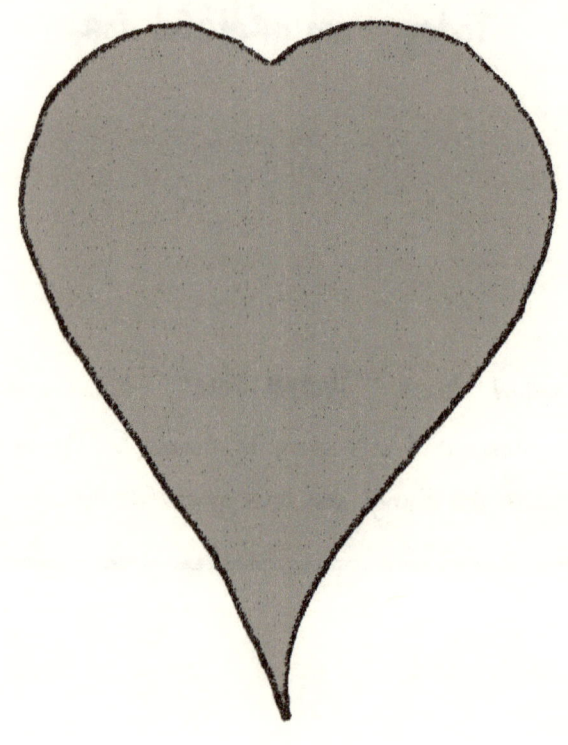

Date: ____/____/____   Day: 53

AN ATTITUDE OF GRATITUDE.

Today, I am grateful for:

1. _____

2. _____

3. _____

In the box below, draw **"Thank You"**. Allow your creativity and love to flow, and it's okay to doodle.☺ While you draw, genuinely thank the things you are grateful for.

Date: ____/____/____   Day: 54

AN ATTITUDE OF GRATITUDE.

Today, I am grateful for:

1. _____

2. _____

3. _____

In the box below, draw **"Thank You"**. Allow your creativity and love to flow, and it's okay to doodle.☺ While you draw, genuinely thank the things you are grateful for.

Date: ___/___/___   Day: 55

AN ATTITUDE OF GRATITUDE.

Today, I am grateful for:

1. _____

2. _____

3. _____

In the box below, draw **"Thank You"**. Allow your creativity and love to flow, and it's okay to doodle.☺ While you draw, genuinely thank the things you are grateful for.

"Gratitude doesn't change the scenery. It merely washes clean the glass you look through so you can clearly see the colors." - **RICHELLE E. GOODRICH**

Date: ___/___/___   Day: 56

AN ATTITUDE OF GRATITUDE.

Today, I am grateful for:

1. _____

2. _____

3. _____

In the box below, draw **"Thank You"**. Allow your creativity and love to flow, and it's okay to doodle. ☺ While you draw, genuinely thank the things you are grateful for.

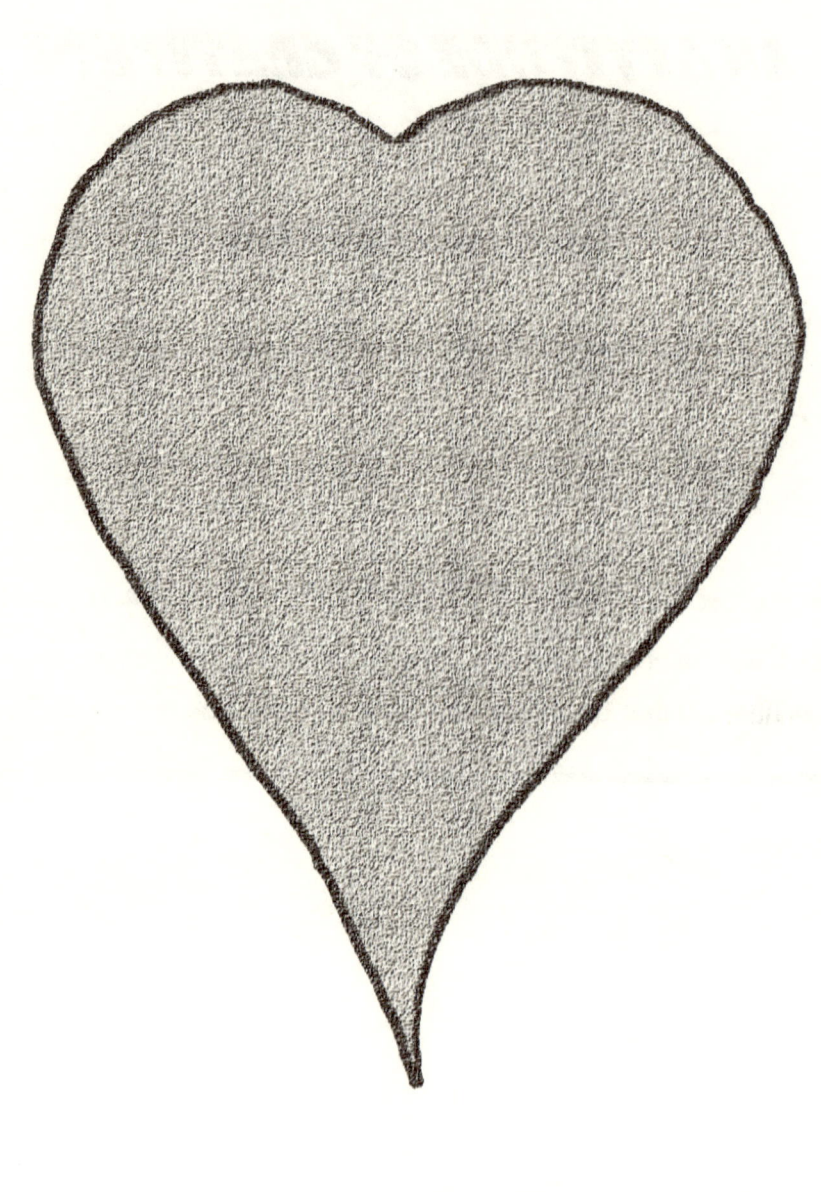

Date: ___/___/___   Day: 57

AN ATTITUDE OF GRATITUDE.

Today, I am grateful for:

1. _____

2. _____

3. _____

In the box below, draw **"Thank You"**. Allow your creativity and love to flow, and it's okay to doodle. ☺ While you draw, genuinely thank the things you are grateful for.

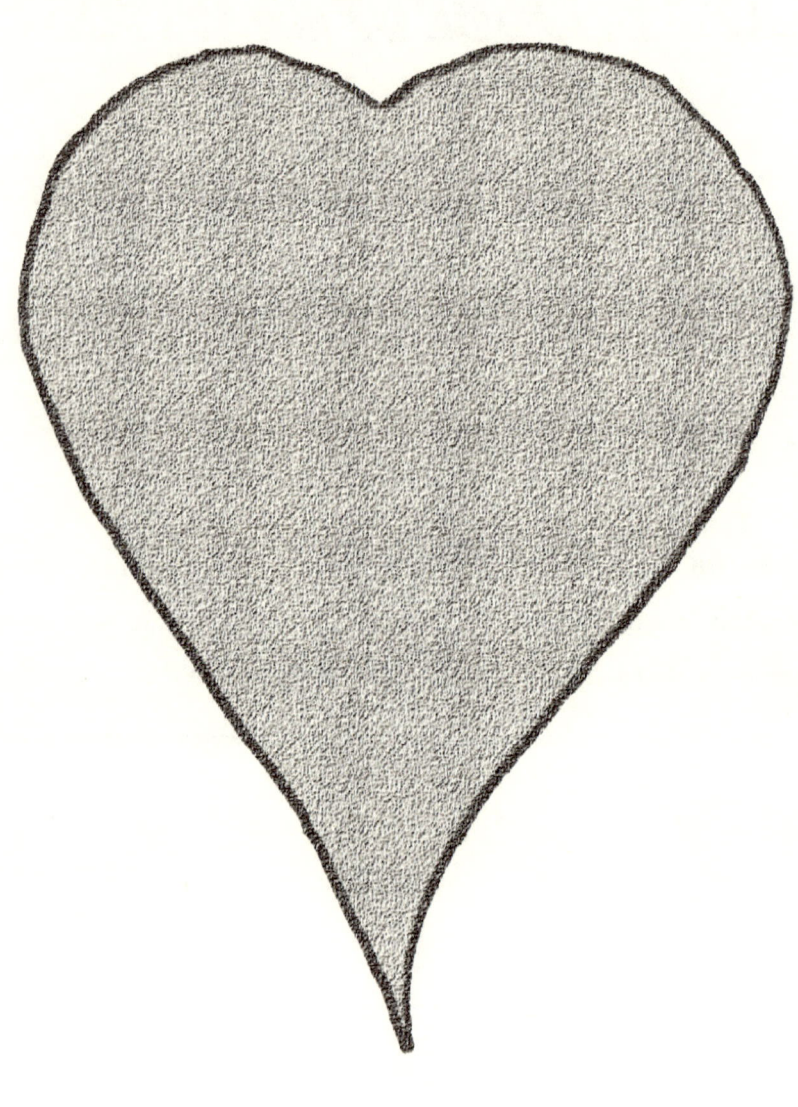

Date: ____/____/____ Day: 58

AN ATTITUDE OF GRATITUDE.

Today, I am grateful for:

1. _____

2. _____

3. _____

In the box below, draw **"Thank You"**. Allow your creativity and love to flow, and it's okay to doodle. ☺ While you draw, genuinely thank the things you are grateful for.

"Gratitude for the seemingly insignificant a seed this plants the giant miracle." - **ANN VOSKAMP**

Date: ____/____/____ Day: 59

AN ATTITUDE OF GRATITUDE.

Today, I am grateful for:

1. _____

2. _____

3. _____

In the box below, draw **"Thank You"**. Allow your creativity and love to flow, and it's okay to doodle. ☺ While you draw, genuinely thank the things you are grateful for.

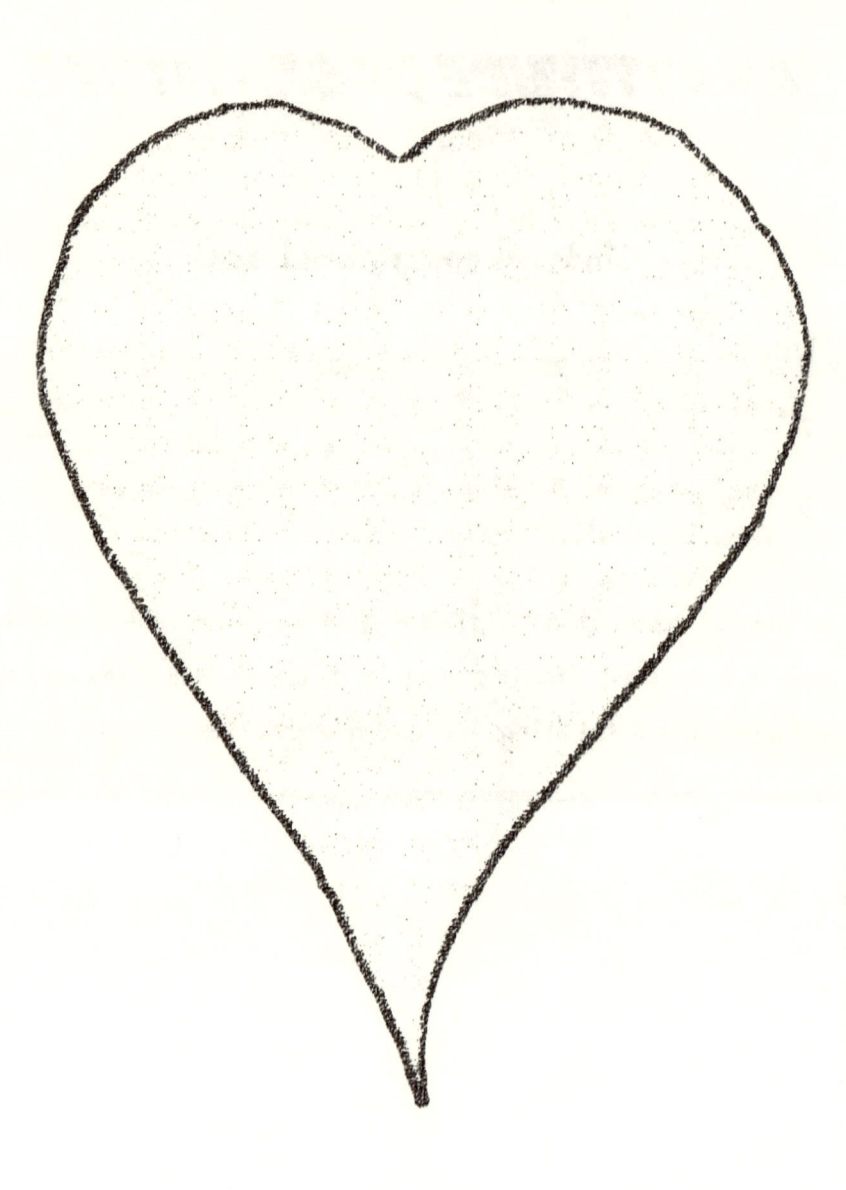

Date: ____/____/____   Day: 60

AN ATTITUDE OF GRATITUDE.

Today, I am grateful for:

1. _____

2. _____

3. _____

In the box below, draw **"Thank You"**. Allow your creativity and love to flow, and it's okay to doodle. ☺ While you draw, genuinely thank the things you are grateful for.

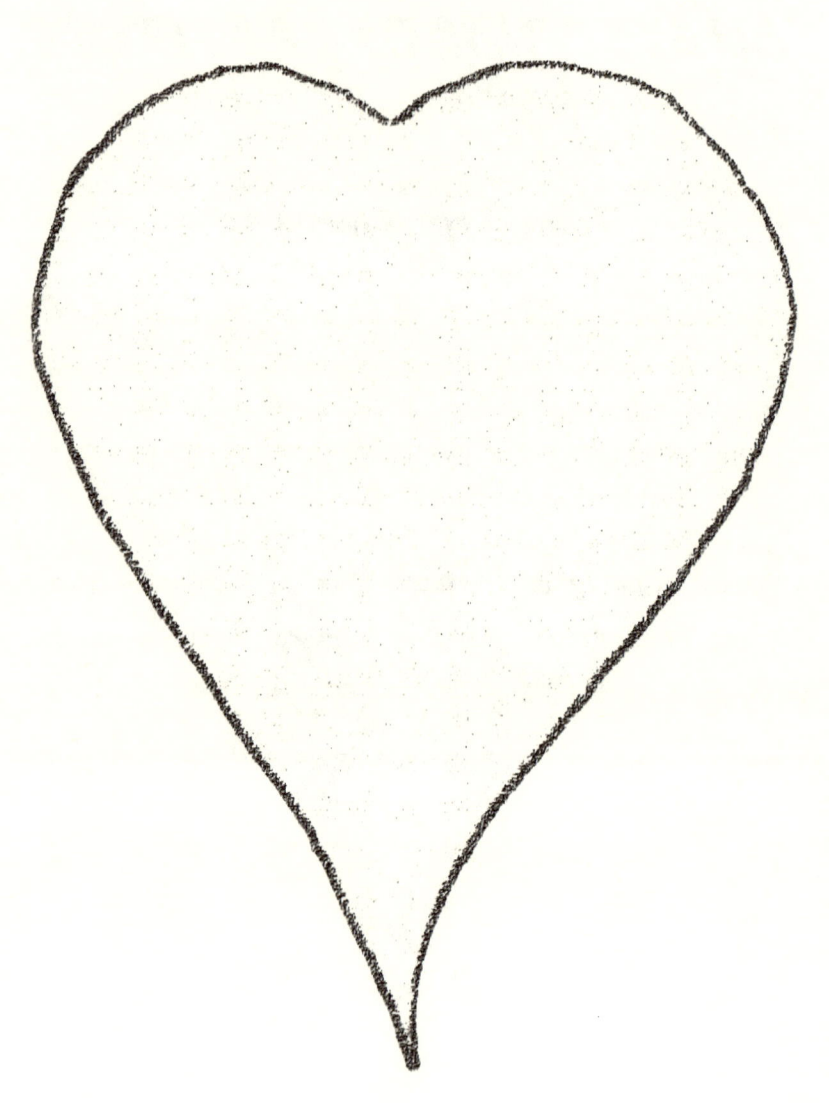

Date: ____/____/____ Day: 61

AN ATTITUDE OF GRATITUDE.

Today, I am grateful for:

1. _____

2. _____

3. _____

In the box below, draw **"Thank You"**. Allow your creativity and love to flow, and it's okay to doodle. ☺ While you draw, genuinely thank the things you are grateful for.

"We can only be said to be alive in those moments when our hearts are conscious of our treasures." - **THORNTON WILDER**

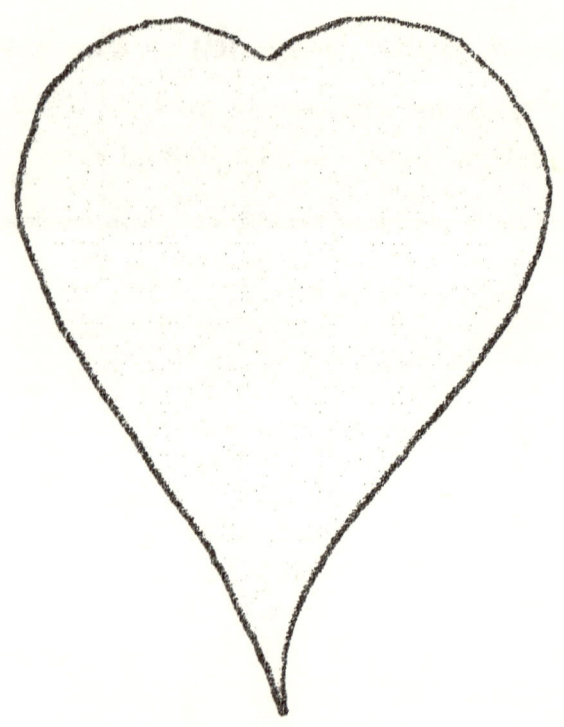

Date: ___/___/___   Day: 62

AN ATTITUDE OF GRATITUDE.

Today, I am grateful for:

1. _____

2. _____

3. _____

In the box below, draw **"Thank You"**. Allow your creativity and love to flow, and it's okay to doodle. ☺ While you draw, genuinely thank the things you are grateful for.

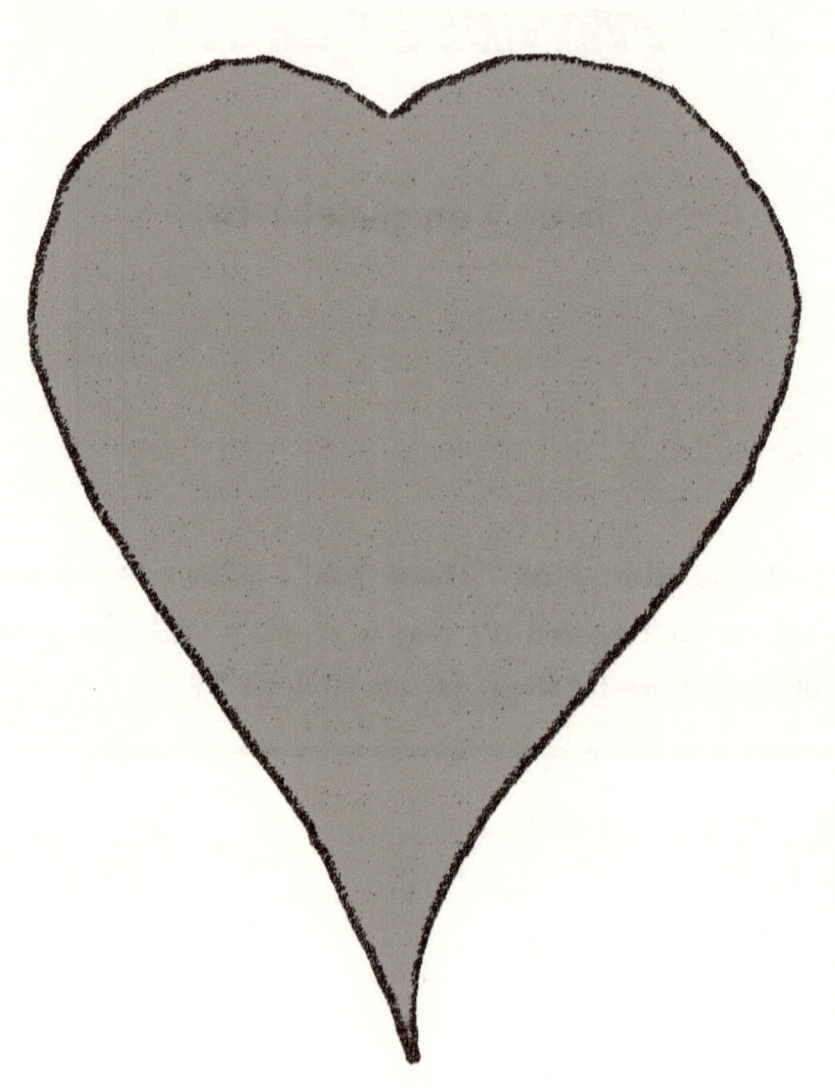

Date: ____/____/____   Day: 63

AN ATTITUDE OF GRATITUDE.

Today, I am grateful for:

1. _____

2. _____

3. _____

In the box below, draw **"Thank You"**. Allow your creativity and love to flow, and it's okay to doodle. ☺ While you draw, genuinely thank the things you are grateful for.

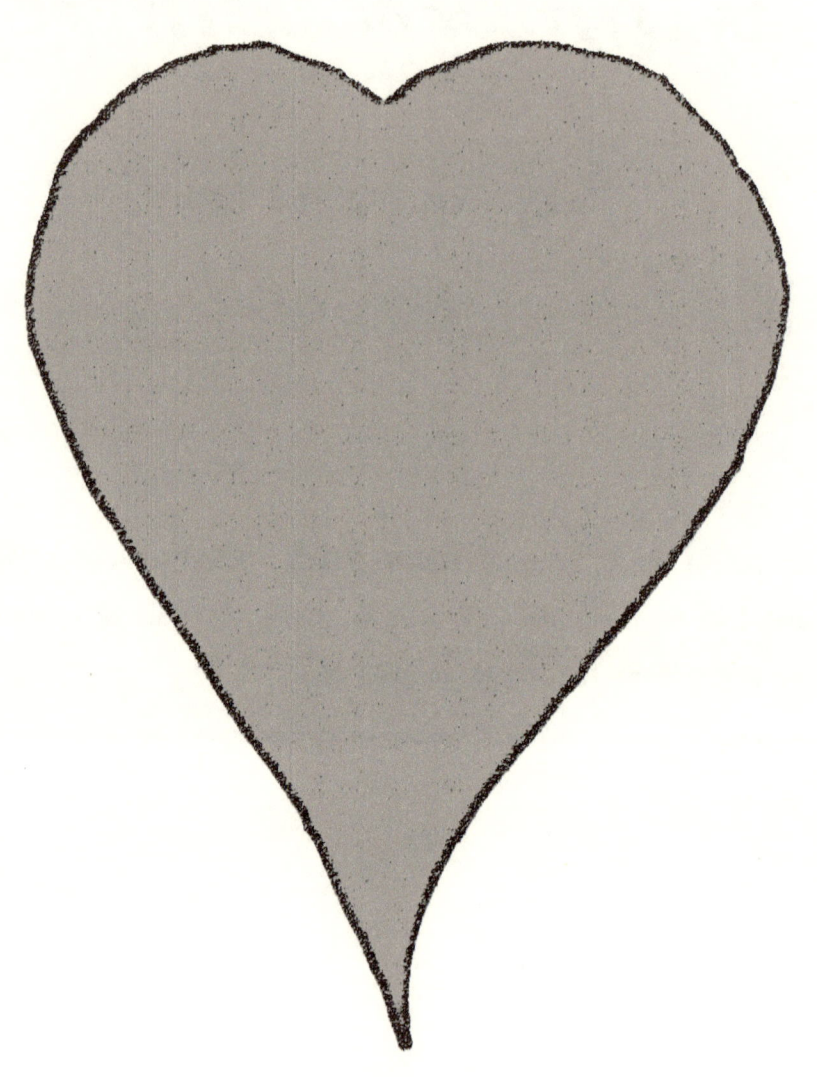

Date: ____/____/____ Day: 64

AN ATTITUDE OF GRATITUDE.

Today, I am grateful for:

1.

2.

3.

In the box below, draw **"Thank You"**. Allow your creativity and love to flow, and it's okay to doodle. ☺ While you draw, genuinely thank the things you are grateful for.

"As we express our gratitude, we must never forget that the highest appreciation is not to utter words, but to live by them."
- **JOHN F. KENNEDY**

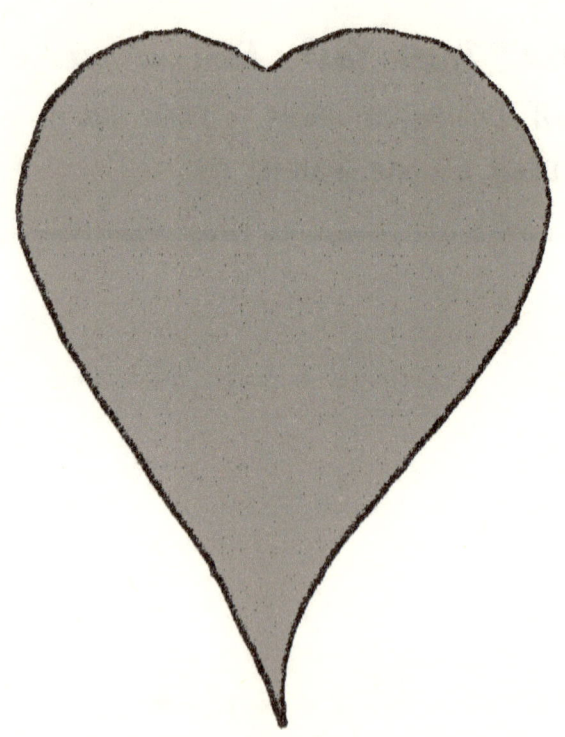

Date: ____/____/____ Day: 65

AN ATTITUDE OF GRATITUDE.

Today, I am grateful for:

1. _____

2. _____

3. _____

In the box below, draw **"Thank You"**. Allow your creativity and love to flow, and it's okay to doodle. ☺ While you draw, genuinely thank the things you are grateful for.

Date: ___/___/___ Day: 66

AN ATTITUDE OF GRATITUDE.

Today, I am grateful for:

1. _____

2. _____

3. _____

In the box below, draw **"Thank You"**. Allow your creativity and love to flow, and it's okay to doodle. ☺ While you draw, genuinely thank the things you are grateful for.

Date: ____/____/____   Day: 67

AN ATTITUDE OF GRATITUDE.

Today, I am grateful for:

1. _____

2. _____

3. _____

In the box below, draw **"Thank You"**. Allow your creativity and love to flow, and it's okay to doodle. ☺ While you draw, genuinely thank the things you are grateful for.

"Gratitude puts us in harmony with the very source that's breathing us, the very power that gives us life." - **MARY MORRISSEY**

Date: ___/___/___   Day: 68

AN ATTITUDE OF GRATITUDE.

Today, I am grateful for:

1. _____

2. _____

3. _____

In the box below, draw **"Thank You"**. Allow your creativity and love to flow, and it's okay to doodle. ☺ While you draw, genuinely thank the things you are grateful for.

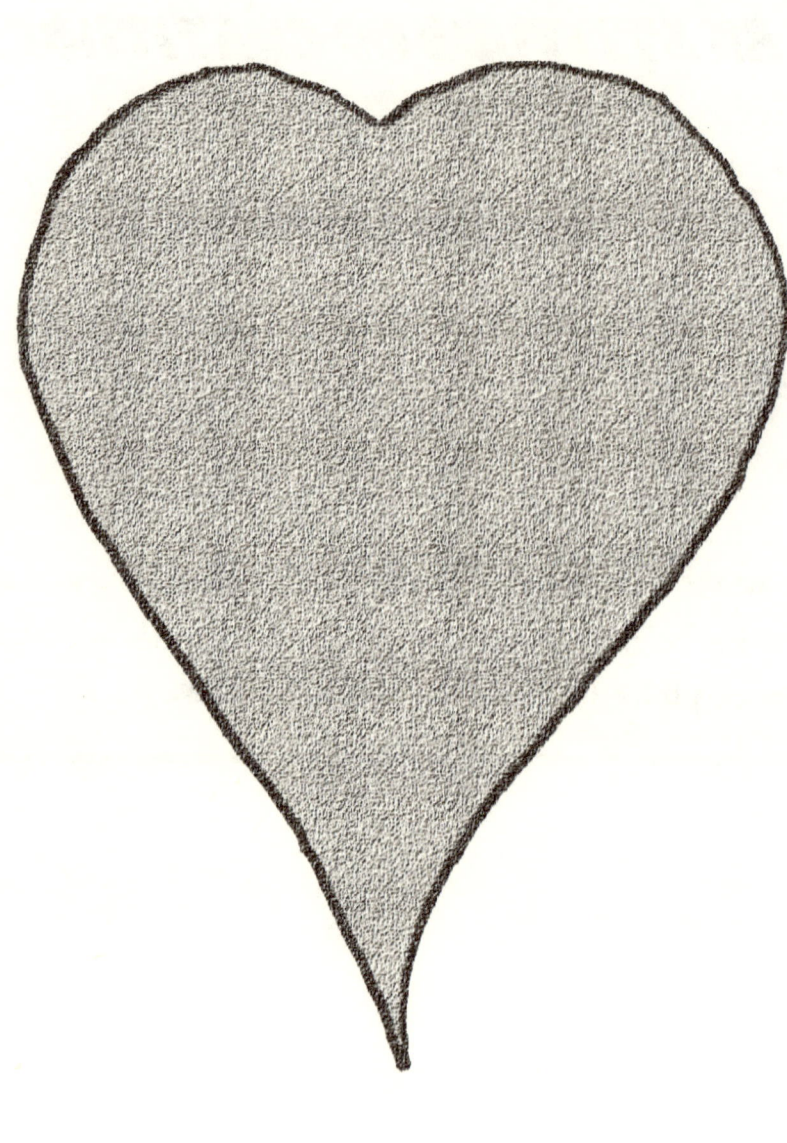

Date: ___/___/___   Day: 69

AN ATTITUDE OF GRATITUDE.

Today, I am grateful for:

1. _____

2. _____

3. _____

In the box below, draw **"Thank You"**. Allow your creativity and love to flow, and it's okay to doodle. ☺ While you draw, genuinely thank the things you are grateful for.

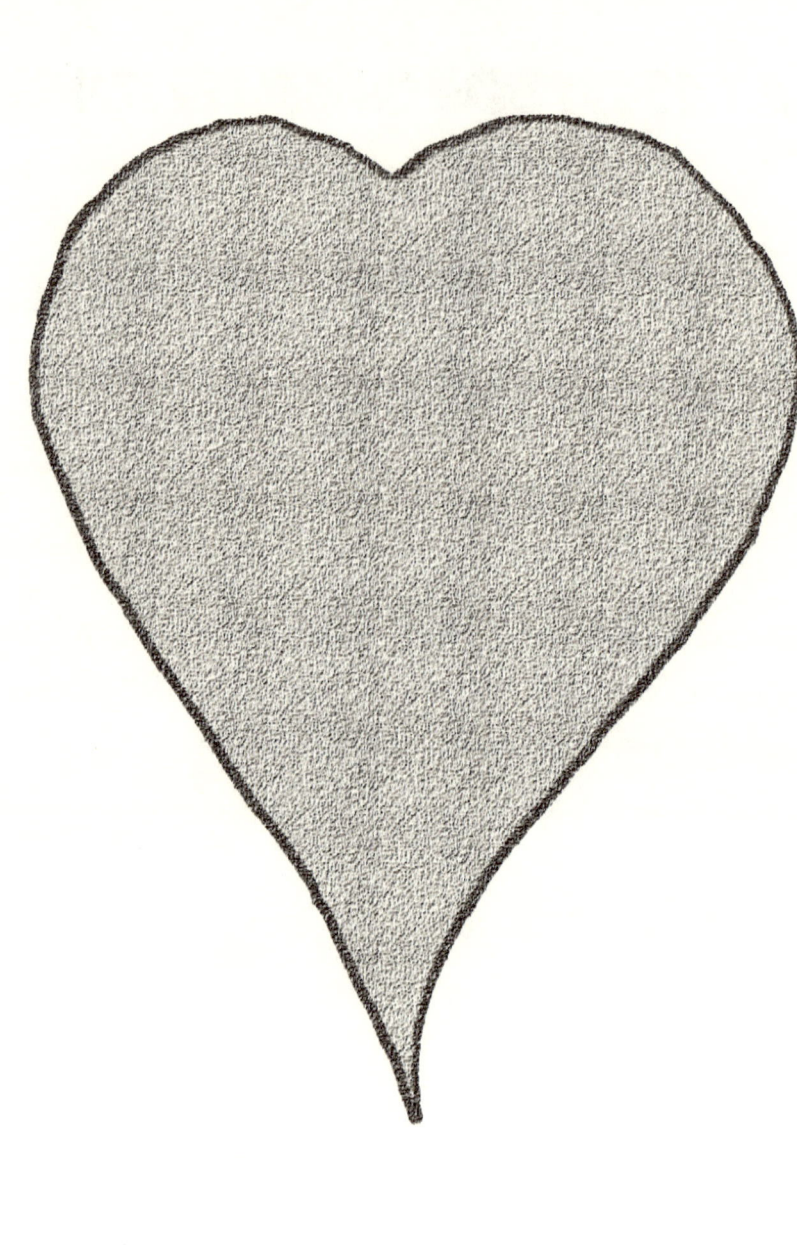

Date: ___/___/___ Day: 70

AN ATTITUDE OF GRATITUDE.

Today, I am grateful for:

1. _____

2. _____

3. _____

In the box below, draw **"Thank You"**. Allow your creativity and love to flow, and it's okay to doodle. ☺ While you draw, genuinely thank the things you are grateful for.

"Let gratitude be the pillow upon which you kneel to say your nightly prayer. And let faith be the bridge you build to overcome evil and welcome good." - MAYA ANGELOU

Date: ___/___/___ Day: 71

AN ATTITUDE OF GRATITUDE.

Today, I am grateful for:

1. _____

2. _____

3. _____

In the box below, draw **"Thank You"**. Allow your creativity and love to flow, and it's okay to doodle.☺ While you draw, genuinely thank the things you are grateful for.

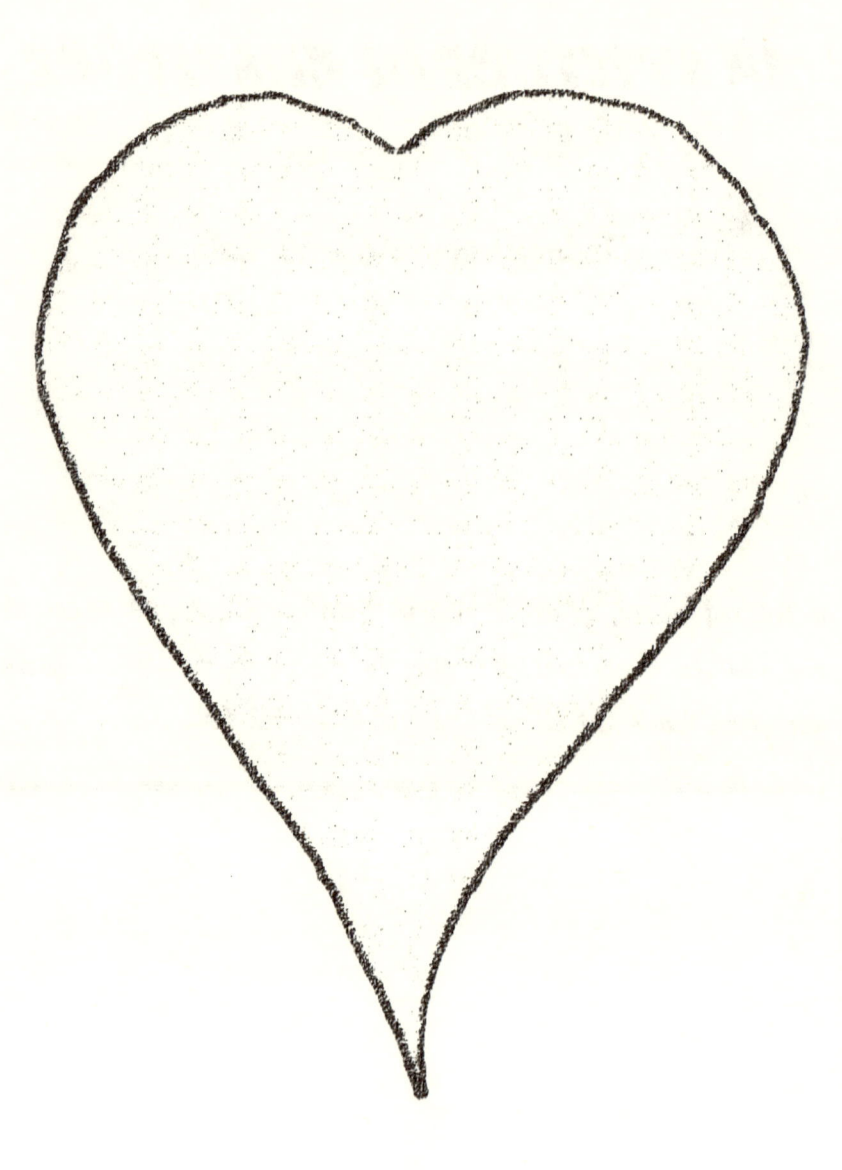

Date: ___/___/___   Day: 72

AN ATTITUDE OF GRATITUDE.

Today, I am grateful for:

1. _____

2. _____

3. _____

In the box below, draw **"Thank You"**. Allow your creativity and love to flow, and it's okay to doodle. ☺ While you draw, genuinely thank the things you are grateful for.

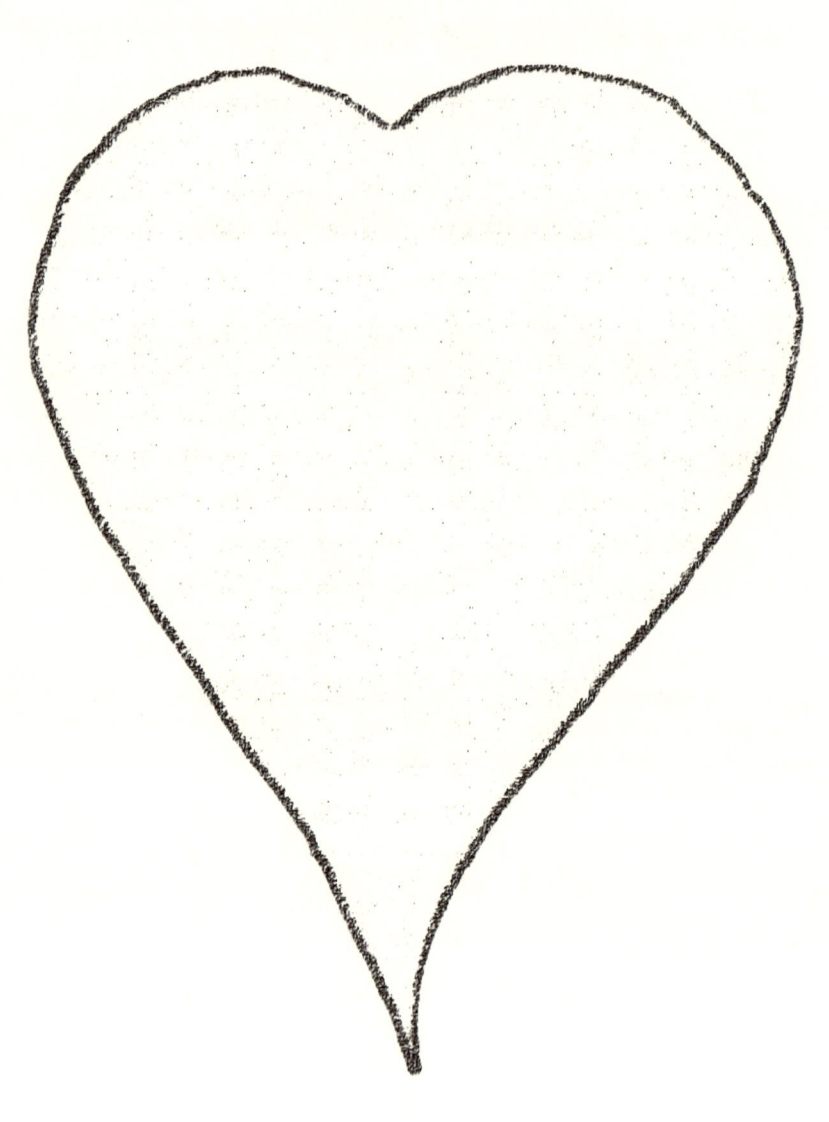

Date: ___/___/___   Day: 73

AN ATTITUDE OF GRATITUDE.

Today, I am grateful for:

1. _____

2. _____

3. _____

In the box below, draw **"Thank You"**. Allow your creativity and love to flow, and it's okay to doodle. ☺ While you draw, genuinely thank the things you are grateful for.

"We often take for granted the very things that most deserve our gratitude." - CYNTHIA OZICK

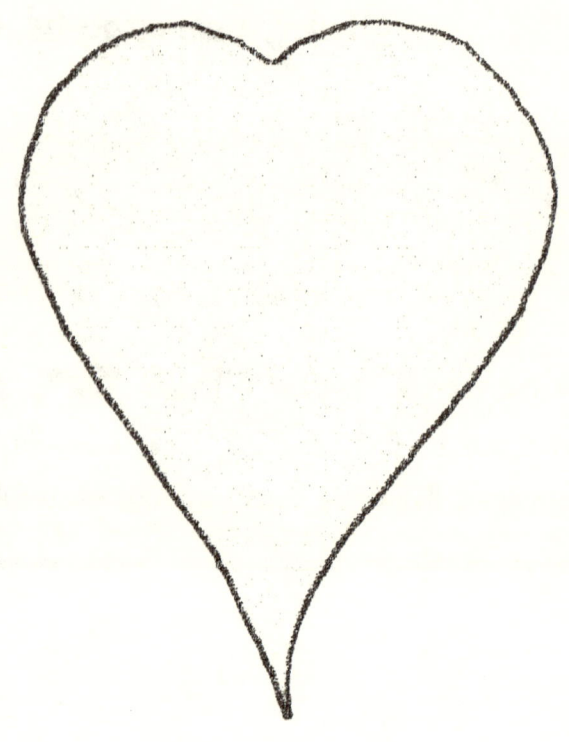

Date: ____/____/____   Day: 74

AN ATTITUDE OF GRATITUDE.

Today, I am grateful for:

1. _____

2. _____

3. _____

In the box below, draw **"Thank You"**. Allow your creativity and love to flow, and it's okay to doodle. ☺ While you draw, genuinely thank the things you are grateful for.

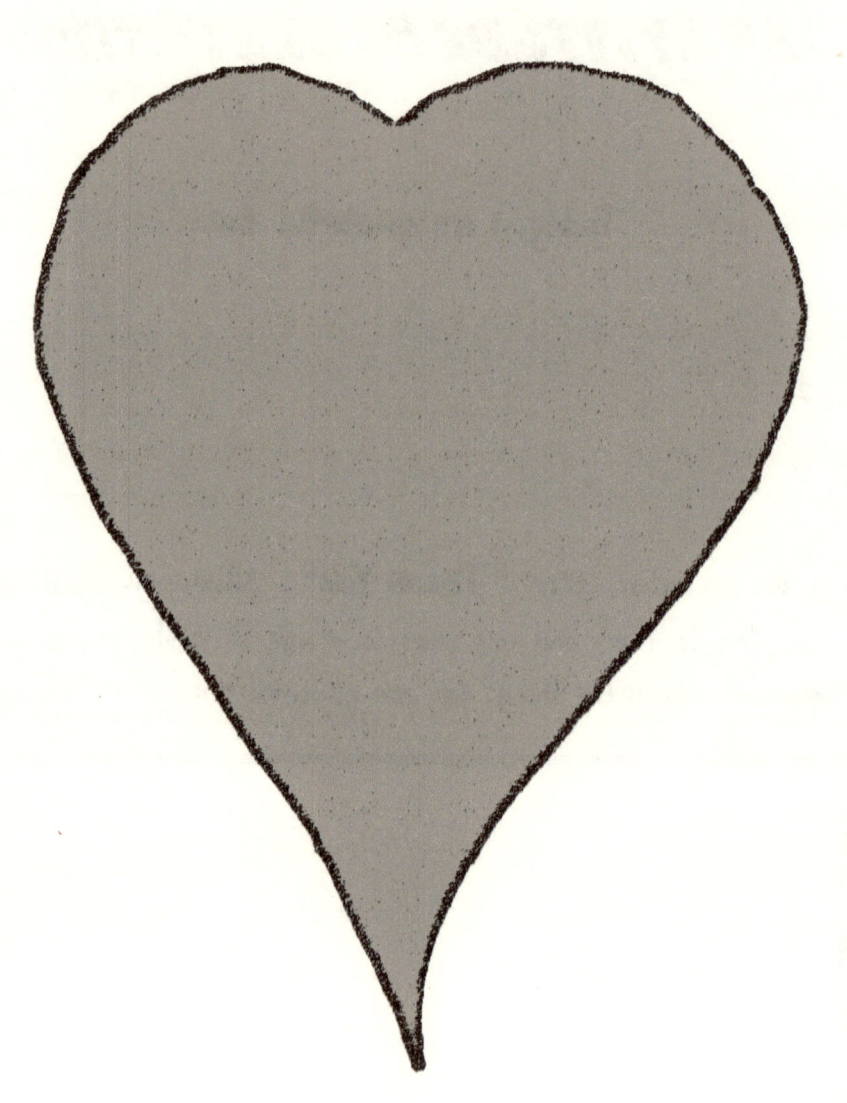

Date: ____/____/____   Day: 75

AN ATTITUDE OF GRATITUDE.

Today, I am grateful for:

1. _____
2. _____
3. _____

In the box below, draw **"Thank You"**. Allow your creativity and love to flow, and it's okay to doodle. ☺ While you draw, genuinely thank the things you are grateful for.

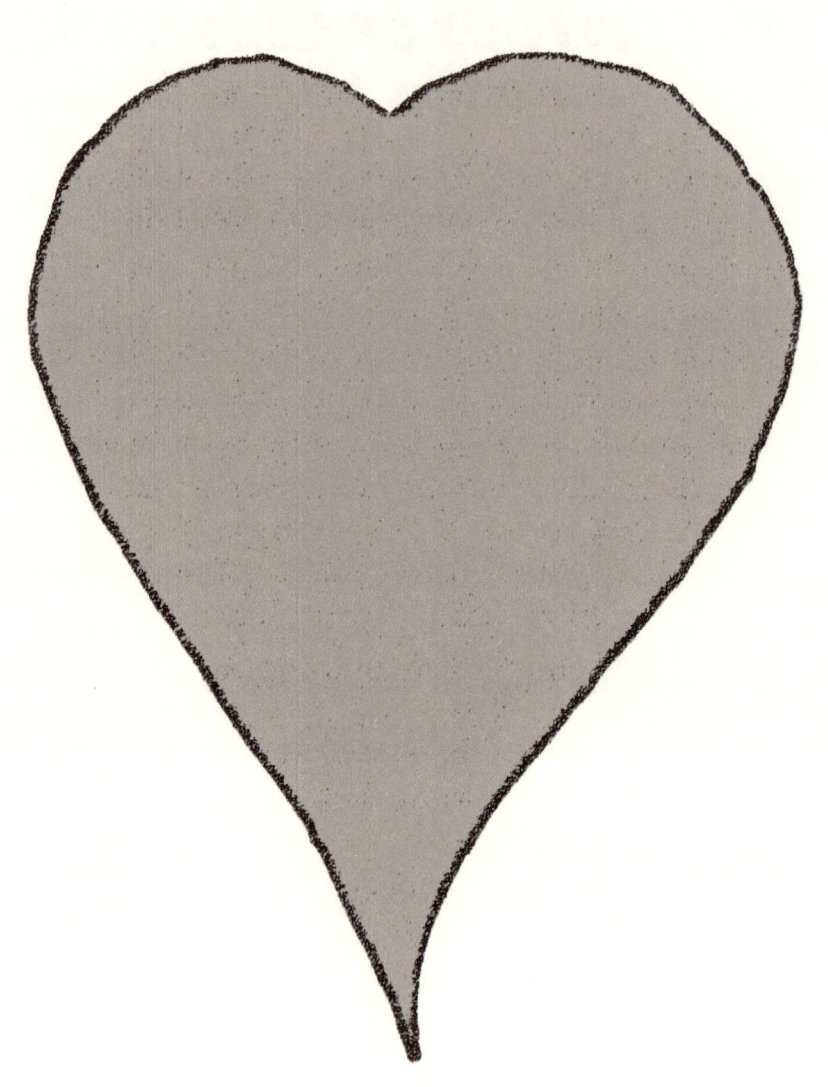

Date: ____/____/____   Day: 76

AN ATTITUDE OF GRATITUDE.

Today, I am grateful for:

1. _____

2. _____

3. _____

In the box below, draw **"Thank You"**. Allow your creativity and love to flow, and it's okay to doodle. ☺ While you draw, genuinely thank the things you are grateful for.

"For your heart is like a flower as it grows, and it's the rain, not just the sun that helps it bloom." - **CHARLES FINK**

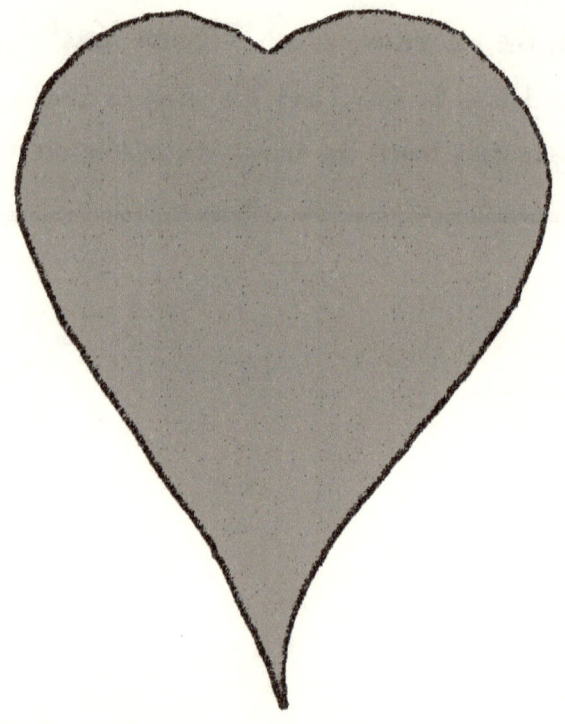

Date: ____/____/____   Day: 77

AN ATTITUDE OF GRATITUDE.

Today, I am grateful for:

1. _____

2. _____

3. _____

In the box below, draw **"Thank You"**. Allow your creativity and love to flow, and it's okay to doodle. ☺ While you draw, genuinely thank the things you are grateful for.

Date: ___/___/___ Day: 78

AN ATTITUDE OF GRATITUDE.

Today, I am grateful for:

1. _____

2. _____

3. _____

In the box below, draw **"Thank You"**. Allow your creativity and love to flow, and it's okay to doodle. ☺ While you draw, genuinely thank the things you are grateful for.

Date: ____/____/____   Day: 79

AN ATTITUDE OF GRATITUDE.

Today, I am grateful for:

1. _____

2. _____

3. _____

In the box below, draw **"Thank You"**. Allow your creativity and love to flow, and it's okay to doodle. ☺ While you draw, genuinely thank the things you are grateful for.

"When I started counting my blessings, my whole life turned around." - **WILLIE NELSON**

Date: ___/___/___　　　　　　　　　　　　　Day: 80

AN ATTITUDE OF GRATITUDE.

Today, I am grateful for:

1. _____

2. _____

3. _____

In the box below, draw **"Thank You"**. Allow your creativity and love to flow, and it's okay to doodle. ☺ While you draw, genuinely thank the things you are grateful for.

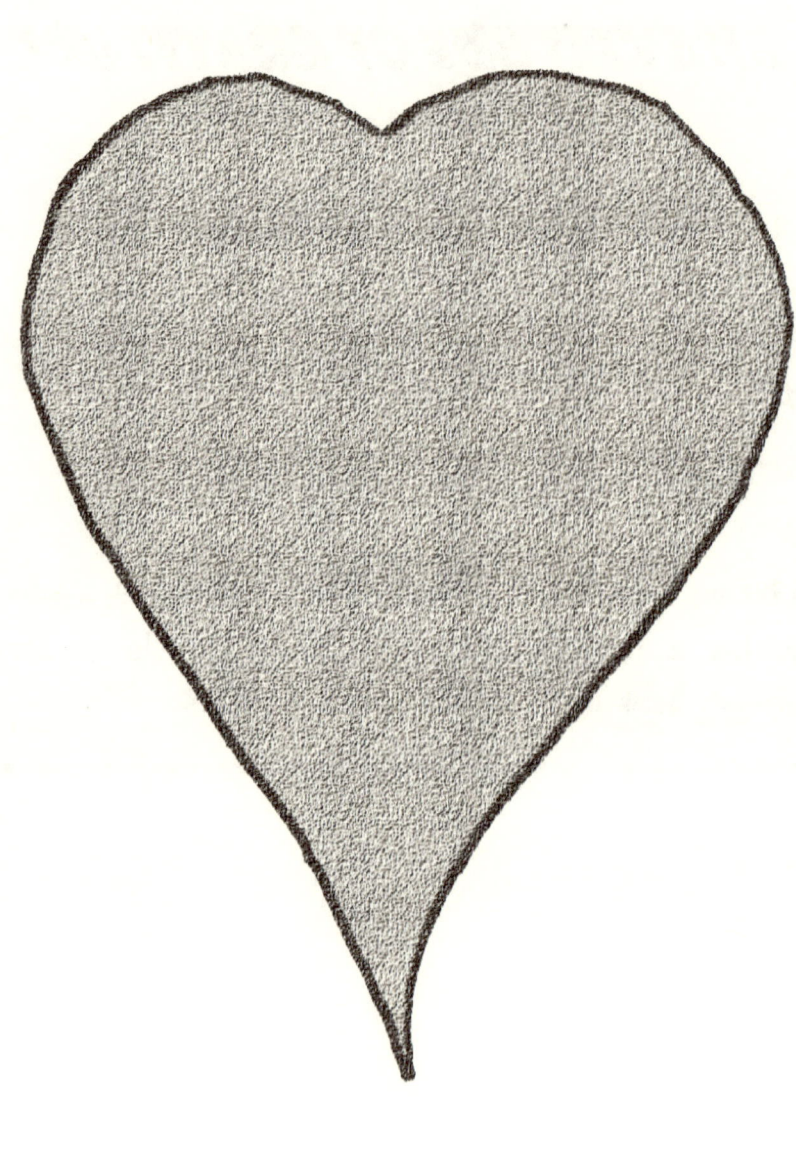

Date: ___/___/___   Day: 81

AN ATTITUDE OF GRATITUDE.

Today, I am grateful for:

1. _____

2. _____

3. _____

In the box below, draw **"Thank You"**. Allow your creativity and love to flow, and it's okay to doodle.☺ While you draw, genuinely thank the things you are grateful for.

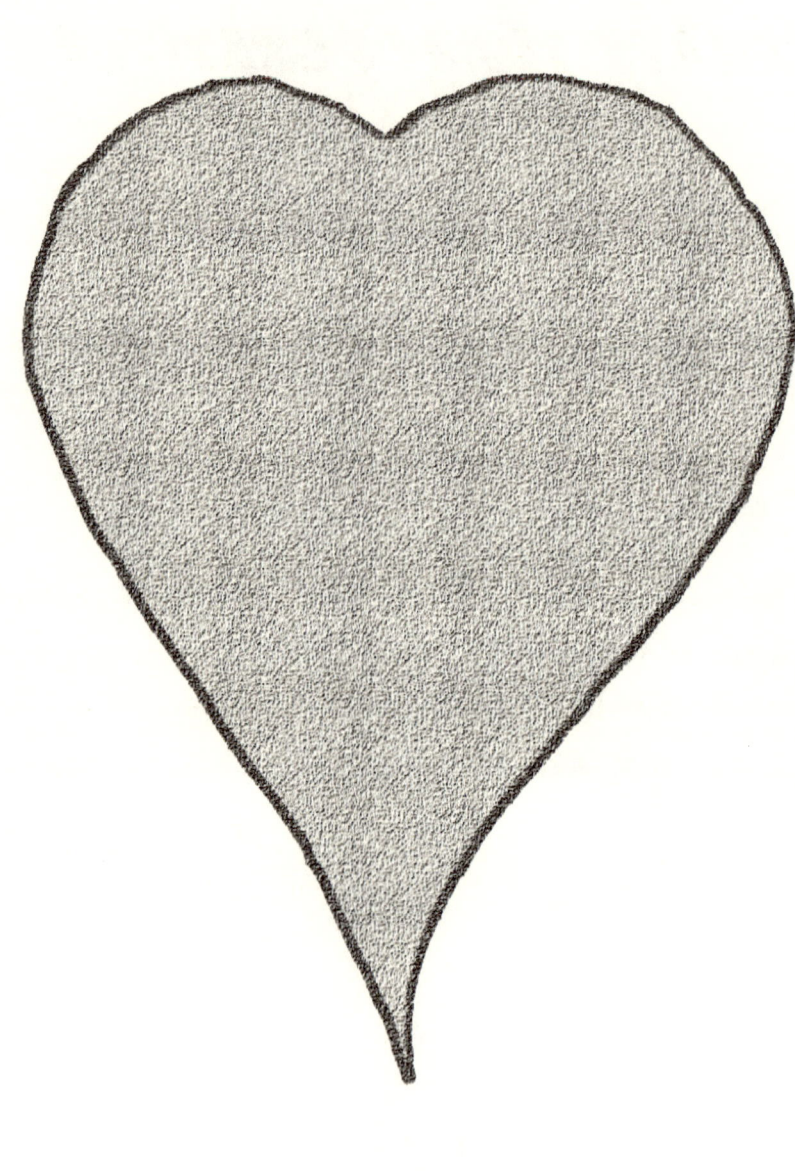

Date: ____/____/____ Day: 82

AN ATTITUDE OF GRATITUDE.

Today, I am grateful for:

1. _____

2. _____

3. _____

In the box below, draw **"Thank You"**. Allow your creativity and love to flow, and it's okay to doodle. ☺ While you draw, genuinely thank the things you are grateful for.

"The more grateful I am, the more beauty I see." - **MARY DAVIS**

Date: ____/____/____ Day: 83

AN ATTITUDE OF GRATITUDE.

Today, I am grateful for:

1. _____

2. _____

3. _____

In the box below, draw **"Thank You"**. Allow your creativity and love to flow, and it's okay to doodle.☺ While you draw, genuinely thank the things you are grateful for.

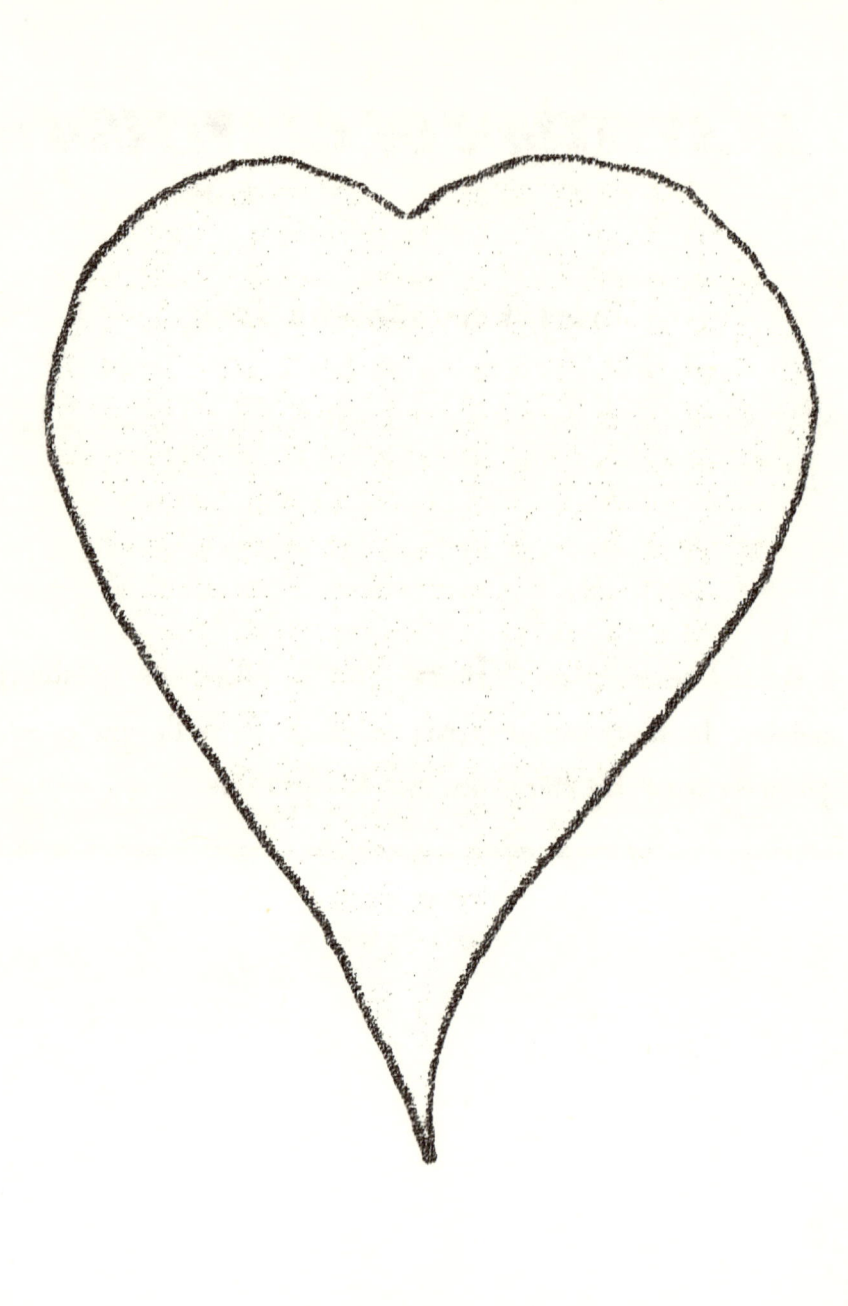

Date: ____/____/____ Day: 84

AN ATTITUDE OF GRATITUDE.

Today, I am grateful for:

1. _____
2. _____
3. _____

In the box below, draw **"Thank You"**. Allow your creativity and love to flow, and it's okay to doodle. ☺ While you draw, genuinely thank the things you are grateful for.

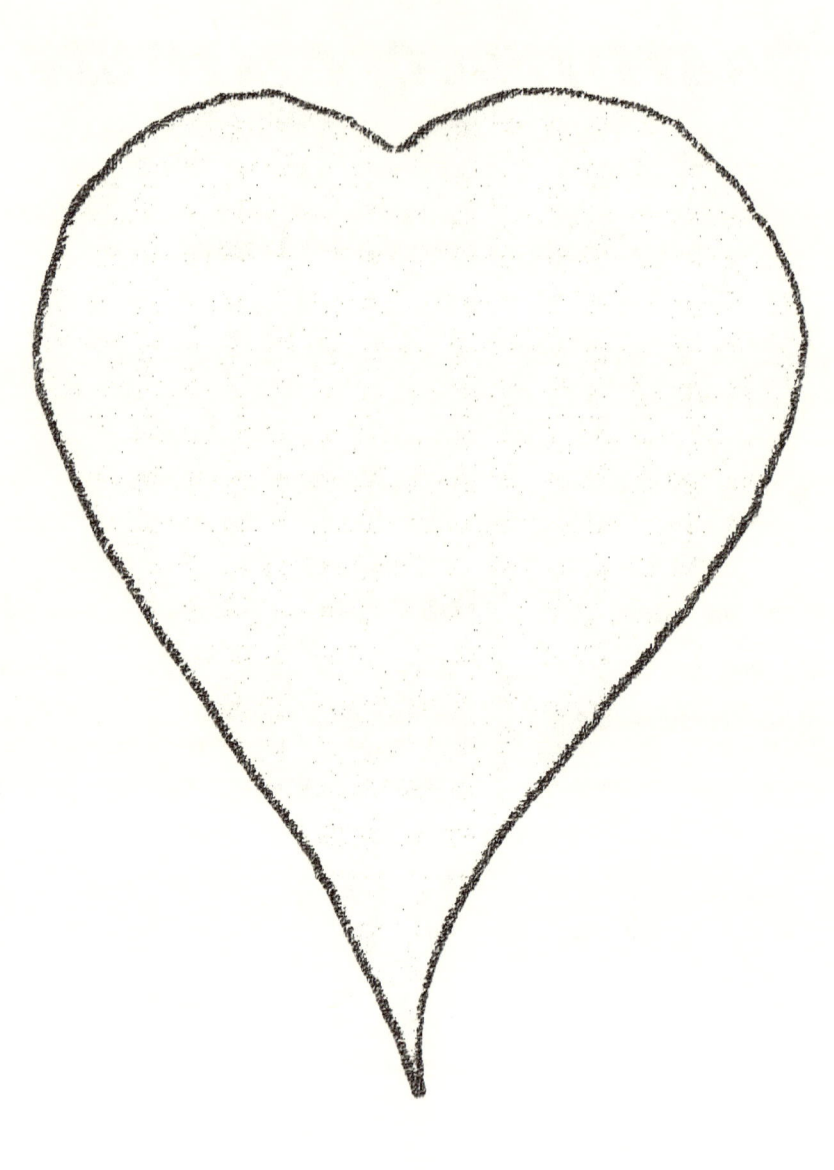

Date: ____/____/____ Day: 85

AN ATTITUDE OF GRATITUDE.

Today, I am grateful for:

1. _____

2. _____

3. _____

In the box below, draw **"Thank You"**. Allow your creativity and love to flow, and it's okay to doodle. ☺ While you draw, genuinely thank the things you are grateful for.

"Gratitude opens the door to the power, the wisdom, the creativity of the universe. You open the door through gratitude." - **DEEPAK CHOPRA**

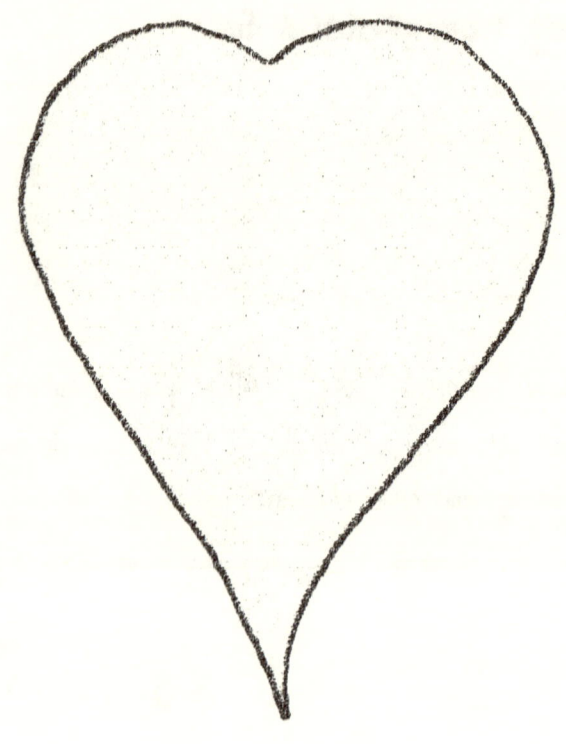

Date: ____/____/____   Day: 86

AN ATTITUDE OF GRATITUDE.

Today, I am grateful for:

1. _____

2. _____

3. _____

In the box below, draw **"Thank You"**. Allow your creativity and love to flow, and it's okay to doodle. ☺ While you draw, genuinely thank the things you are grateful for.

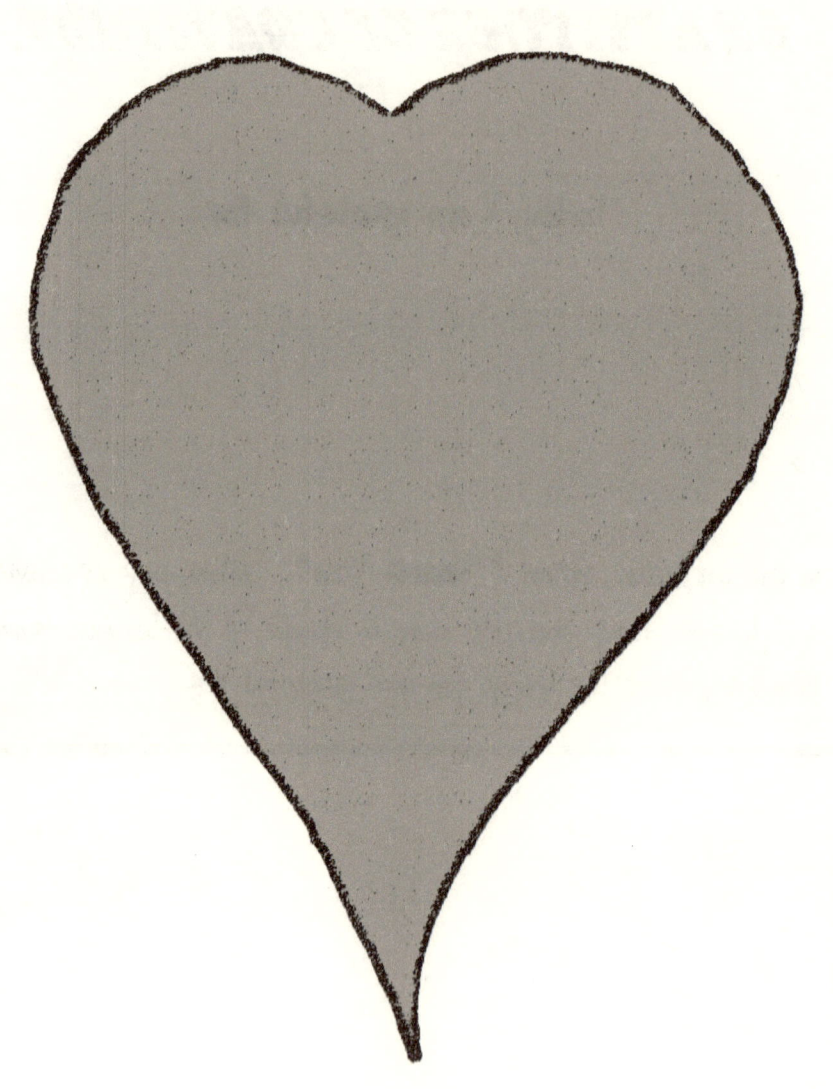

Date: ____/____/____   Day: 87

AN ATTITUDE OF GRATITUDE.

Today, I am grateful for:

1. _____

2. _____

3. _____

In the box below, draw **"Thank You"**. Allow your creativity and love to flow, and it's okay to doodle. ☺ While you draw, genuinely thank the things you are grateful for.

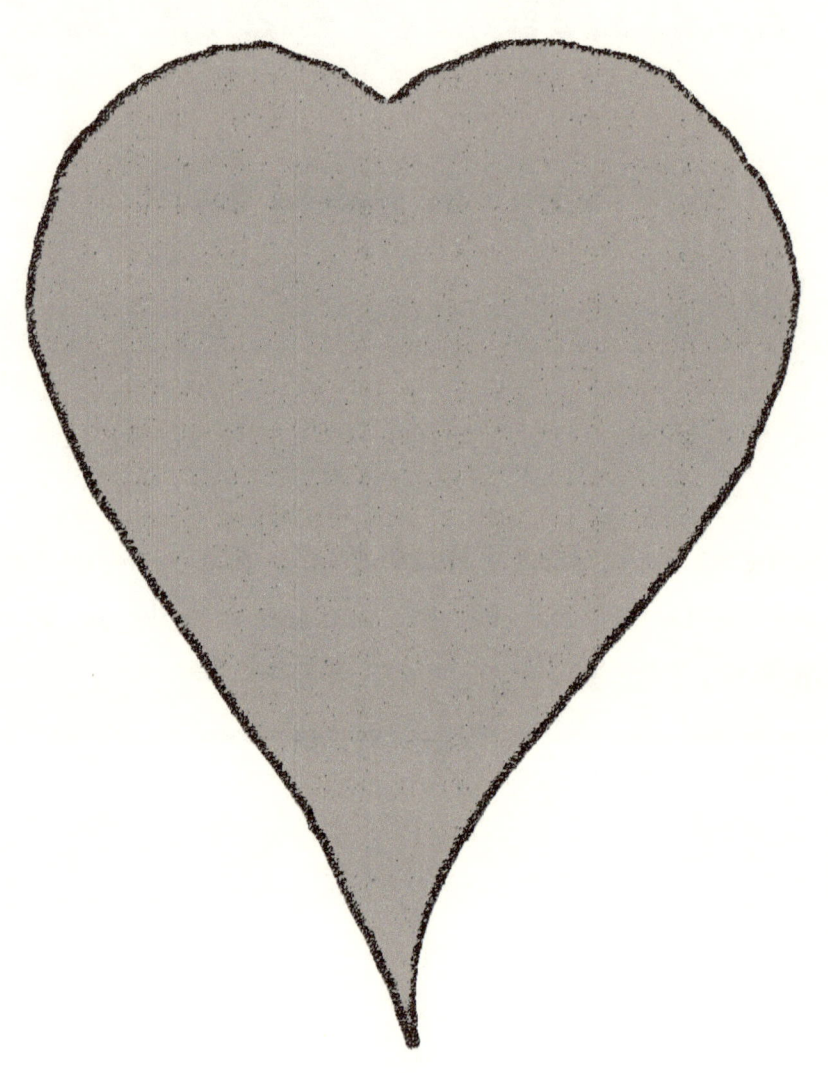

Date: ____/____/____   Day: 88

AN ATTITUDE OF GRATITUDE.

Today, I am grateful for:

1. _____

2. _____

3. _____

In the box below, draw **"Thank You"**. Allow your creativity and love to flow, and it's okay to doodle. ☺ While you draw, genuinely thank the things you are grateful for.

"Dwell on the beauty of life. Watch the stars, and see yourself running with them." - **MARCUS AURELIUS**

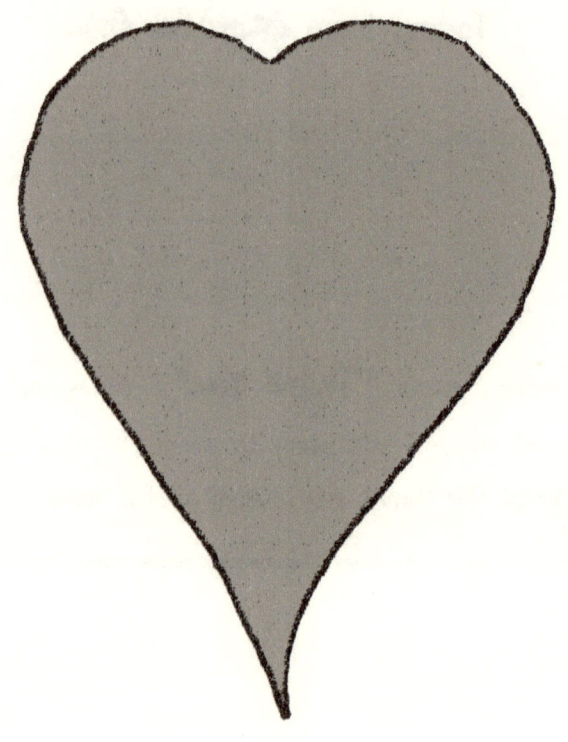

Date: ____/____/____   Day: 89

AN ATTITUDE OF GRATITUDE.

Today, I am grateful for:

1. _____

2. _____

3. _____

In the box below, draw **"Thank You"**. Allow your creativity and love to flow, and it's okay to doodle. ☺ While you draw, genuinely thank the things you are grateful for.

Date: ____/____/____   Day: 90

AN ATTITUDE OF GRATITUDE.

Today, I am grateful for:

1. _____

2. _____

3. _____

In the box below, draw **"Thank You"**. Allow your creativity and love to flow, and it's okay to doodle. ☺ While you draw, genuinely thank the things you are grateful for.

GRATITUDE LETTER

It's time to write a brief gratitude letter. Use the space provided. A gratitude letter will further assist you cultivate an attitude of gratitude. Write a gratitude letter to someone in your life that you are grateful for.

> "At times, our own light goes out and is rekindled by a spark from another person. Each of us has cause to think with deep gratitude of those who have lighted the flame within us." **- Albert Schweitzer**

Congratulations! You completed 90 days of gratitude. How do you feel? I hope it's better than when you began this journey.

As a reward for completing 90 days, I'd like to reveal a method of attracting success and abundance. This technique was taught by Yogananda and shared in his booklet, "The Law of Abundance". Supposedly, Steve Jobs applied this method.

According to Yogananda, inner peace and joy attract success and abundance, and this is so because peace and joy are Godly and success and abundance come from The Source. With this is mind, the first step in the procedure to attract success and abundance is to generate a state of inner peace and joy. To do so, meditate until a sense of peace and joy is felt. (Fortunately, you've completed 90 days and you're prime to quickly enter a state of peace and joy).

After a sense of inner peace and joy is achieved, thank The Source for what you have. After which ask The Father to teach that The Source is the power behind all wealth and the value in all things. Finally, state something such as the following: I and The Source are one.

Genuinely repeat this process a few times a day for 30 days.

The opportunities and ideas to increase your success and abundance will then arrive. Receive the opportunities and ideas, and when exploring them, remain peaceful and joyous. And remember to work hard and stay the course.

Yogananda recommends that if this method is successful, a person donate 10% to God and 6% to humanity. A common reason for this method failing is an inability to routinely remain peaceful and joyous.

If 90 days of gratitude was a benefit to you, consider undertaking another 90 days. Good luck!

> "Acknowledging the good that you already have in your life is the foundation for all abundance."
> - Eckhart Tolle

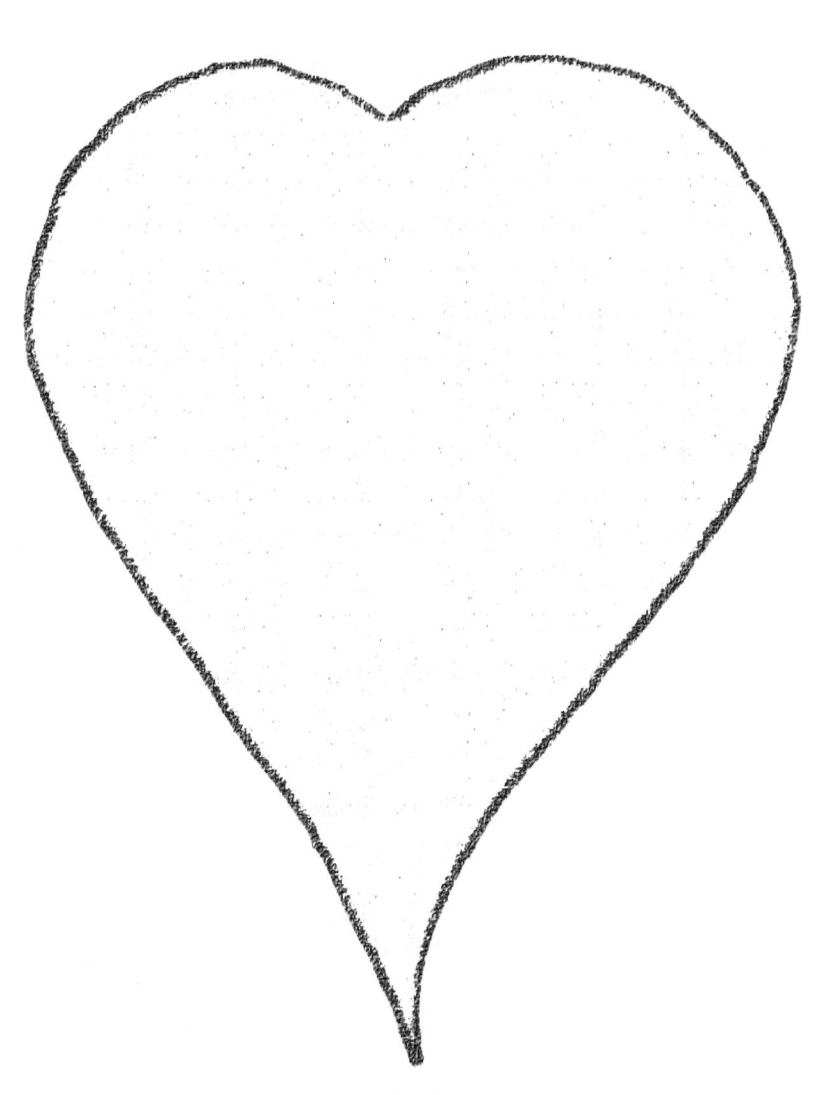

BOOKS BY MIKE BHANGU

 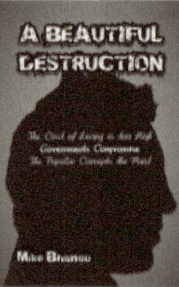